ALSO BY NORA McINERNY

It's Okay to Laugh (Crying Is Cool Too)
No Happy Endings: A Memoir
The Hot Young Widows Club
Bad Moms: The Novel

BAD VIBES ONLY

(AND OTHER THINGS I BRING TO THE TABLE)

ESSAYS

NORA McINERNY

ONE SIGNAL
PUBLISHERS

ATRIA

New York London Toronto Sydney New Delhi

ONE SIGNAL
PUBLISHERS

ATRIA

An Imprint of Simon & Schuster, Inc.
1230 Avenue of the Americas
New York, NY 10020

Copyright © 2022 by Nora McInerny

Some names and identifying characteristics have been changed.

First One Signal Publishers/Atria Books hardcover edition October 2022

ONE SIGNAL PUBLISHERS / ATRIA BOOKS and colophon
are trademarks of Simon & Schuster, Inc.

For information about special discounts for bulk purchases, please
contact Simon & Schuster Special Sales at 1-866-506-1949 or
business@simonandschuster.com.

The Simon & Schuster Speakers Bureau can bring authors to your live
event. For more information or to book an event, contact the Simon &
Schuster Speakers Bureau at 1-866-248-3049 or visit our website at
www.simonspeakers.com.

Manufactured in China

1   3   5   7   9   10   8   6   4   2

Library of Congress Cataloging-in-Publication Data has been applied for.

ISBN 978-1-9821-8671-5
ISBN 978-1-9821-8673-9 (ebook)

For The Terribles.

I've never been a natural, all I do is try, try, try.
—TAYLOR SWIFT, "MIRRORBALL"

CONTENTS

Before We Begin

When my son was two years old, he would greet new children at the park by saying, "I'm Ralphie! My dad is dead!" The children tended not to care very much about Ralph's deceased father, but any parent or caregiver around them would freeze, trying to will their faces to project an air of inquisitiveness rather than anguish.

"Yes!" I'd say. "That's correct!" And the two of us would go about our business, which meant me standing at the bottom of a slide Ralph would never go down, while he stood at the top and made sure every other kid got a turn. Some days I might offer an insincere apology to the person whose day seemed to be ruined by the facts of Ralph's and my life, and some days I might even offer up the tidbits I could sense they were craving: *How did he die? How old was he? Did he deserve it?*

If you're craving those same tidbits, I don't blame you. And the answers are: Brain Cancer. Thirty-five. And no, not even a little bit. Ralph's limited vocabulary and sense of social norms had freed him from the tyranny of conversational niceties and allowed him to state the facts, however awful they be. Soon enough, I knew, he would learn to lie like the rest of us: by omission, by wrapping the unruly threads of his life tight, or trimming them off entirely. He will learn that the best way to keep people comfortable is to hide your own discomfort or deny it entirely. He will learn to fake it until he makes it, to betray himself in a million ways, just like his mother.

I don't know when I learned that "fine" was the correct answer to "how are you?" but nobody ever had to explicitly tell me that "well, I'm teetering on the edge of a nervous break-down" is definitely not the answer your colleague is looking for while you pass each other in the hallways between your many overlapping meetings. It doesn't take a psychology de-gree to understand that some things are just *more pleasant* than others, and that as comfort-seeking mammals with dis-posable income we are attracted to the pleasant, the easy.

And yes, we know that "life is hard," but we also really want it to be hard in ways that are manageable and more in-convenient than difficult. We want our setbacks to be setting us up for comebacks, and more than anything, we want to be able to alchemize our pain into something shiny and *good*: a lesson learned, a warning sign for others. Our suffering is just a vehicle for our self-improvement.

Ha.

"Good Vibes Only" makes a cute saying for a mug, but a pretty ominous interpersonal standard. My bookshelves and credit card statements will tell you that I've tried my best to smooth all my rough edges, to master my own mind and attract the kind of life I want. Depending on the aperture, it might look like I've done it: I have a handsome (second) husband named Matthew and a blended family of four chil-dren, and our holiday cards (which arrive after the holidays) are printed on thick cardstock and sometimes feature professional photos. But a family can only blend when other family units have fallen apart, and five out of six of the people smiling at you from that card are still sorting through the residual trauma of what was lost before this was gained.

I don't put that on the back of the card, but maybe I should. The vibes out here are a mixed bag, and mostly out of our control, like the economic forces that determine who can pay their rent and who lives in an encampment on the side of the freeway, or the random multiplication of cells that showed up as a brain tumor in my first husband's handsome head.

I don't want to live in a world where the *only* vibes are bad, but I cannot stay for long in a room where the only vibes allowed are the pleasant ones, either. I was a child who lay in bed crying about pain I hadn't yet experienced—like the deaths of my very alive parents, who were doing the *New York Times* crossword puzzle in bed down the hall—and a teenager who read Carson McCullers. I was also a child who delighted in physical comedy and fantasized about growing up to marry Chris Farley (may he Rest in Peace). I grew up to be an adult whose job is to speak to strangers about the hardest things they've been through, to help them tell the truth about their own discomfort so that other strangers can learn to be comfortable with the discomfort of others in the comfort of wherever they listen to podcasts. And I also grew up to be an adult with an abiding passion for early aughts reality television, a die-hard Swiftie, and the kind of person who—regrettably— ends phone calls by saying "smell ya later."

I have always been the saddest happy person I know (or

maybe the happiest sad person I know), the middle part of a Venn diagram that I'd caption The Life of The Party Pooper.

There are plenty of books out there promising you a better version of your life, books where the author uses their own narrow personal experiences to offer universal advice to the reader. Those books sell very well, and most of them are on my bookshelves. But this book is for people who cannot help but put a little sprinkle of sadness on their happiest memories, or who know that life is short and *still* fill those waking hours with long-held grudges against former colleagues whose names they cannot recall. I welcome and respect all of your vibes. Here are some of mine.

1

It Hurts to Be Beautiful

The woman standing in front of me with a syringe has a question. She is holding an iPad opened to a PDF document informing me about the risks of this procedure, and I've scrolled through it to get to the small box that declares "I understand the risks," which I click without hesitation, swiping my finger across the screen to approximate my signature.

I'm proudly middle-aged, though that seems to rile up anyone older than me. I've spent nights in hospital beds and afternoons in chemo infusion rooms. Surrounded by the sick, I have felt a new appreciation for my healthy body: the miracle of my two lungs and my countless cells, every piece of me working in harmony together to sustain this life of mine. Aging is a gift, the goal of everything my body does for me, thanklessly, day and night. I want to experience aging in all its fullness. I do not, however, want to look it. I feel a slight pinch, experience a bit of redness, and in two weeks I see those lines relax and disappear.

Is this:

1. Self-care
2. A submission to patriarchal beauty standards that require women to cling to their youth
3. An exercise in futility
4. All of the above
5. None of the above

I came of age in what may be the tackiest era of female beauty: the late 1990s and early 2000s. The turn of that century brought major enhancements in the accentuation of femininity, and a celebration of the effort. The Playboy to Prime Time pipeline was filled with silicone: Pamela Anderson's breast implants bouncing slowly and dramatically in her tiny red bathing suit during the opening credits of *Baywatch*, Jenny McCarthy's chest pulling against her baby tees on *Singled Out*. I wasn't allowed to watch either of these things, but I learned how to turn off the TV the moment my parents hit the garage door opener, sprinting up the stairs and into my bed with an open book as if I'd whiled away the after-school hours getting lost in American History instead of soaking in the much sexier American Present. I was built like a two-by-four and dressed like an extra in *The Mighty Ducks*, but I knew beauty when I saw it. It was in a bottle of bleach and boobs that looked like overfilled water balloons. It was in my mother, who barely wore makeup when I was a child other than the silver tubes of Clinique lipstick she kept in every bag and tucked into the glove compartment of her car: a sheer, berry purple that made her naturally thick lips look like candy. Mom let her hair air-dry into soft waves and clipped it back. Her hands were long and elegant, and her nails almost always unpainted. Her best accessories were her royal-blue eyes, framed in giant, jewel-toned glasses. Her own mother—who had once been young and lithe and smooth—was now completely shapeless, a sexless pile of bones and organs coated in a thin layer of tissue paper–skin. Her face looked as though my own mother's had been wadded up and left at the bottom of a pile of damp laundry, her ice-blue eyes peering through drooped eyelids and her teeth stained by years of coffee and cigarettes and red wine. She wore free men's T-shirts with ankle-length skirts printed with loud florals and stained with the clay she shaped into bowls and pitchers in the shed behind her cabin.

For me, there was no competition between this kind of beauty and the kind I saw on television and in magazines, no hierarchy or value attached to them. But there is one, of course, and it whiplashes us between standards: the "natural" beauty whose appeal is so innate she doesn't need any assistance . . . and those that are fakes, facsimiles. Effort is dismissed as artifice, but I've always seen it as an art to be able to transform yourself so fully. Natural beauty is a gift bestowed on a few whose features fall within the fickle standards of the time, but even natural beauty requires some effort. I have spent hundreds of dollars on a brand of beauty products modeled exclusively by poreless teens that promises a "natural dewiness" that my own skin can no longer produce. Celebrities will claim that their beauty secrets are simply sleep and water and "good nutrition," without mentioning the thousands of dollars they've spent on laser treatments and hair removal and hair extensions and a full-time glam squad.

Even when it is their job to look good, they feel compelled to pretend it just *happens*, erasing the hours and the dollars it took to create the look that normals will attempt to re-create in the aisles of Target.

Taylor Swift wrote "I've never been a natural, all I do is try, try, try." And while I do not think she was talking about injectables, I hear in her lyrics the pressure to exude effortlessness. To openly strive and reach—to show your work, whether it is seeking higher office or flaunting your obvious plastic surgery—is to be distrusted, to be false. To not try at all—to let your armpit hair grow down to your waist or your skin wrinkle like a raisin, to let your body stay soft and squishy after a baby—is also suspect. There's no good way to be a woman.

I felt an almost instant sense of shame after my first injection, and every one thereafter. When complimented on my appearance, do I disclose that I've cheated? *Have* I cheated? Where did I cross the line between effortless natural beauty and effortful deception? Was it when I fought the natural darkening of my blond hair with a head full of platinum highlights in ninth grade? When I baked in tanning booths after signing a waiver acknowledging that yes, a high-wattage light bulb might cause cancer? Was it when I sat in poorly ventilated nail salons while my technician wore an N95 mask and coated the keratin that grows from my fingertips in various forms of pigmented chemicals? Was the line crossed when I had small false eyelashes glued to my own, or when I purchased long strands of human hair in thick wefts stitched into my own locks? Was it when I struggled into underwear that eliminated the slight bulge of my lower intestine and uterus so that skirts would sit smoothly on my curveless body?

It Hurts to Be Beautiful

. . .

At five years old, my cousin Lillian and I were given the gift of a lifetime: a few dollars apiece to spend at the mall in my small town, a glamorous building that had a fountain, an escalator, and a Claire's. Claire's was—is, maybe still—the closest thing that young girls have to a dream store. As an adult, you may find your peace of mind wandering the aisles of Target or Sephora, or by snatching up your most coveted items at the Nordstrom sale. But as a little girl in the late 1980s with five dollars burning a hole in your pocket, there was no better place to shop than Claire's, a small box of a store packed from floor to ceiling with various accessories designed to thrill and excite: small post earrings with peace signs, puffy headbands covered in sequins, a fanny pack? All this and more awaited Lillian and me on the other end of a twenty-minute ride in the way back of my mother's Volvo.

Like many little girls, Lillian and I were desperate to be mistaken for twins. Mistaken is the wrong word, because we were constantly trying to con people into *thinking* we were twins, saying natural things like "Hey, twin? Where is Mom?" while eyeing the strangers around us like, *Yeah, did you hear that? We are twins,* and prepared to counter any questions like "Why don't you look alike?" with snappy comebacks like "Ever heard of *fraternal twins separated at birth, you half-wit?*" It goes without saying (although of course we say it repeatedly while sitting in what is essentially the trunk of the car) that we'll need whatever we buy on this day to be *matching,* and after testing my mother's patience by begging her to let us get our ears pierced by an untrained sixteen-year-old girl in rural Minnesota, we decided on matching pairs of red enamel heart earrings with a screw-on back.

These are our first and only accessories, and we act as though they are precious diamonds, not a metal that we are probably allergic to. We take turns trying to clamp each other's little earlobes in between the two small pads, cranking them closer together. "Tighter!" we scream at each other. "It might fall off!" We study our faces in my family's hall mirror, our earlobes throbbing with the pressure.

"Do your ears hurt?" I ask Lillian, trying not to cry.

"A little," she lies. "But it hurts to be beautiful!"

Now, our pain was meaningful and holy. If this was the cost of beauty, we were happy to pay it, baby! We had the rest of the afternoon to spend however we wanted to, which was constantly touching our ears to make sure the earrings were still there and tightening them until my mom noticed our earlobes were purple and unscrewed them in a panic, wondering aloud if we might have killed the flesh altogether by cutting off the blood supply. Lillian and I cried not from the threat of possible disfigurement but from the pain of losing our most beautiful feature.

It hurts to be beautiful, and it hurts to lose your beauty, too. I read Nora Ephron's *I Feel Bad About My Neck* before I had a single wrinkle, and yet I knew exactly why she felt bad about her skin loosening, hanging, signaling to the world that she was no longer young. My own beauty has always felt like an avocado: not ripe, not ripe, not ripe . . . and on its way to rotting in the blink of an eye. I spent the better part of my adolescent and teenage years waiting to be desired, desperate to be perceived as beautiful. The first time I experienced what I would now call street harassment was on a family trip to New York City, where a man walked next to me for a block, asking for my number while my oblivious family strolled on ahead. I was *thrilled*. I wrote about it in my journal, noting that he called me "beautiful" and ignoring the fact that he was at least a decade older than me and invading my personal space. Even when I responded with a middle finger, every honk of a horn or shout from a car was also a small shot of affirmation: I was beautiful, not because of my wit or my intellect, but because an unwashed man in a Nissan Altima shouted it from his car window at a stoplight.

Dolly Parton is one of the most talented songwriters in history, a philanthropist whose investment in COVID-19 research hastened the arrival of a vaccine that your high school friend who now sells essential oils is convinced also contains a microchip. She's universally beloved and the subject of podcasts and books and a fanbase that nearly deifies her. Her famous quips, like "It takes a lot of time and money to look this cheap, honey!"[1] or her confession that she modeled her look after the "town tramp," seem to put her ahead of the joke, but the jokes kept coming, seemingly intent on chipping away at her serious accomplishments by amplifying her obsession with something as trivial as her looks. Interviewers including

---

1 Dolly Parton, *Dolly: My Life and Other Unfinished Business* (New York: Harper Collins, 1994).

Oprah and Barbara Walters seemed intent on forcing her to justify them, with Walters telling her in 1977, "You don't have to look like this."

Of course she doesn't! And neither do I!

But I *like* it. I like that my own artifice and effort also allow a certain level of laziness: the eyelashes I wore for a year had me waking up looking like a Disney princess, the Dysport really does make my skin look better even without makeup, and the extensions I wore for a year gave me full, voluminous hair without spending hours styling and piling on products. My deep emotional well is not drained by the shallow pursuit of beauty, and maybe it is even accentuated by it. I'm highly aware that everything is temporary: my life will end, my extensions will loosen, and the neurotoxins will wear off.

I intended to limit my injections to Dysport, some "natural" smoothing and relaxing—maintenance, really—but the woman with the syringe has a pitch for me: Have I thought about dermal filler? I have not, so she explains that with just a few syringes we can fill in my hollow cheeks and weak chin and accentuate the jawline that has slid into my neck over the past year or so. I'm not just intrigued but excited, and tell her to go for it. Fifteen incredibly painful minutes later, she holds a mirror up to my face. Aside from the red welts indicating where the needles have punctured my skin, I don't really see a difference, but I'm assured that in a few weeks, when the filler settles, I'll call and thank her. Instead, electric bolts of pain shoot from my chin up to my still-numb lower lip, which is raw from being accidentally bitten with every meal. I ice it, swallow ibuprofen, and try to stay off Google until the weekend is over and I feel comfortable calling to report my symptoms. Yes, I'm experiencing an unintended form of facial paralysis, but I also don't want to ruin anyone's weekend, ya know?

I return to be injected with another substance that will undo all that was done a few days before, dissolving the filler and relieving the pressure on a nerve that isn't pleased about being crowded with a foreign substance. But weeks later, I am still biting my numb lower lip every time I eat, spicing up every meal and snack with a hint of my own blood. The nerve will take time to heal itself, to bring proper feeling and functionality back to my face.

Matthew makes a light joke one night, after I've howled in pain at my incisor piercing my inner lip yet again.

"The free version of your face worked fine, didn't it?"

I laugh, not because his joke is any good, but because the joke's on him: he's never known a free version of my face; he only thinks he has. Without this filler, my cheeks will go wherever they want to, I suppose. My jawline will have to be accentuated the old-fashioned way, by layers of contouring makeup and good lighting.

And if I don't regain all the feeling in my lower lip, oh well. I understood the risks.

2

Hello, Me

It took three rapid COVID tests, forty text messages, and three PayPal transfers to get my friends and me together for a weekend away. A *working* weekend away, and not even a weekend but a Wednesday and Thursday, because the home rental was half the price during midweek. Still, we arrived at our temporary home on the outskirts of Joshua Tree, California, with laptops and sweat suits and edibles, prepared to finish the project we'd started an entire year before. Writing as a group is a special kind of magic. Only one person can actually write at a time, so we took turns typing while the other two attempted to be useful. I'm the best typist, but Brandy is the funnier of the three of us, so Jess and I sat impotently at the kitchen table as she tapped away at her keyboard, eating candy and the occasional edible. We took sporadic breaks to sit outside like lizards soaking up the desert sun under SPF 80 and wide-brim sun hats, because in our late thirties, both our egg count and our skin elasticity have taken a nosedive.

"Isn't it funny," Brandy said, her legs dangling from the egg chair that only her four-foot-eleven frame could comfortably fit into, "that we'll never be the kind of women that are, like, classy?" Jess and I—both in oversized T-shirts and bodies that are over five foot ten—blinked.

"Think about it," Brandy said wistfully. "We'll never be a Cate Blanchett or a Kerry Washington. Just . . . think about it."

I wanted to protest, but I was interrupted by the flash of a memory: me, just weeks before, folding all six of my J.Crew wool pencil skirts—yellow, green, blue, pink, red, and black— and lovingly donating them to the local thrift shop. Two of them still had the tags on them, though I know I'd worn them before. Would an elegant woman repeatedly wear clothing that still had the tags attached? I had fully intended to be an elegant woman in pencil skirts, even though my height made walking in a narrow band of fabric absolutely comical, and my creative job made dressing up entirely unnecessary, even before a global pandemic relegated me to a home "office" in my closet. I'd tried to at least look the part sometimes, but always ended up feeling like I was the world's most boring cosplayer, struggling to sit with my knees together and keeping my arms down to conceal the rings of sweat soaking through my top. Still, I hadn't considered that I would *never* be elegant. It felt like a possibility I was just delaying until I had a job as an evening news anchor or could comfortably describe myself as a philanthropist. I looked at myself a little more objectively: my unwashed hair was pinned back from my face, hanging in greasy waves. My sweatpants had sprouted a small hole at the knee. I was wearing . . . crocs. With socks. My car, parked just a few yards away, was coated with white crust from the grackles who had taken over the ficus tree next to our driveway and asserted their dominance over me and my sensible sedan. I'd meant to take it for a wash, but I hadn't.

"Shit," Jess whispered, sniffing her armpits, "you're right." We sat there in stoned silence for hours, possibly minutes, imagining the versions of ourselves that would never be. I dipped briefly into a world where I'm told, "You look just like Carolyn Bessette-Kennedy" so many times that it's embarrassing. A world where all my children's first names are last names, types of trees, or small towns my family settled many generations ago (this has to be a fantasy because my Irish immigrant ancestors landed originally in a town called Lake City, Minnesota, which has absolutely no name potential). In my fantasy, my family has vacationed on the same private island off the coast of Maine for generations, and even though I look like a model (again, embarrassing!), I'm also quite outdoorsy. I probably eat oysters and own candlesticks.

The fantasy fell apart quickly, like all the IKEA beds I've assembled myself after kind of sort of checking the instructions. I would never master a chignon—neither the hairstyle nor the pronunciation—I would not be a woman of mystery and grace but the same Nora whose children's impression of her is a heavy eye roll and a "You gotta be shitting me." Perhaps a part of me—the part who gave up her pencil skirts— had known this already. But what about the other parts of me? The versions of Nora who had ordered magnetic eyelashes, imagining herself to be the kind of woman who could go full glam on a Tuesday, or who had stacked up piles of books by Pema Chödrön, certain she could become quieter, more considerate, less reactive. Were they just as impossible as the Elegant Nora? What about the Nora who went to Burning Man and spent all ten days trying to *not* see all the old penises that were flapping around everywhere she looked under the guise of "performance art"? I'd jettisoned her—and the boyfriend who'd convinced her that trip fell under the definition of "vacation"—but wasn't she tucked inside me somewhere?

At thirty-seven, I hesitate to refer to myself as aging, but I am. I've reached an age where I can recall an event that feels fresh to me—say, attending Burning Man, or being dropped on my ass in front of my friend's entire wedding reception when an enthusiastic groomsman thought he could scoop all six feet of me into his arms—and realize I'm discussing an event that took place a full decade ago. I'm at an age where my own children describe the formative rom-coms of my early adulthood—*Runaway Bride, The Object of My Affection*—as *vintage rom-coms*. Vintage! I'd assumed I was going through my midlife crisis at age thirty-one, which was the halfway point of my own father's life span, but I think that year of accepting and obsessing over my own mortality was just a normal byproduct of grief. What I'm experiencing now is not about death at all but the rapid passing of life itself, illustrated with frequent and jarring realizations that what has been will never be again. Julia Roberts will not hold the same cultural significance for my own children as she did for me, and my daughter will in no way understand the sexual appeal of Richard Gere.

"Life is just going too fast," my second grader wept during one very difficult bedtime. His little brother had just turned four, and while the cake and ice cream were still coursing through his bloodstream, so too was the realization that his brother was getting *older*. "Soon I'll be eight! And then I'll be ten! And then I'll be a grown-up and you'll be dead!" I wanted to say, "If you're *lucky*, I'll be dead when you're a grown-up," but I caught myself and instead just wiped the fat tears from his cheeks. After several minutes of emotional spiraling, he fell asleep, no doubt dreaming about his impending adulthood, which was already slipping through his fingers.

It is ageism to believe that we are running out a clock, that once our youth is behind us, so are the best years of our lives. My youth was personally unremarkable, and I spent a great deal of it stuck in my own sad head. And it is also realistic to accept that our future possibilities are limited, not just by the passing of time but by the decisions and commitments we've made through time. Brandy was right; we will not be elegant women. I will not be a person who builds an expansive country home to summer in with her young children, because my children are already pretty big, and we don't have "summer as a verb" kind of money. Even if we did, I just don't think I have it in me to care about two different houses at once! Just as I will not be skipping off to Paris for three weeks of unencumbered writing time, because my husband is great but *not that great*, and again, the whole money thing. Nor will I own a closet of cream and earth-tone classics that can be mixed and matched to create a wardrobe that makes people wonder, "Has she just never spilled a cup of coffee while trying to carry all of her belongings from the house to the car in one trip?"

The future ahead of me is not boundless, and never was.

Every choice I made eliminated other versions of myself. I wonder often when, specifically, these possible futures evaporated. Was it the moment I placed my hands on either side of a tapped keg, kicking into an assisted handstand while a guy named Brett or maybe Brad placed the nozzle in my mouth and released a stream of Natural Light while a crowd of drunken teenagers counted the seconds (thirty-seven—not to brag!). Maybe she disappeared when I was just fifteen years old, lying on a sanitized recliner in a tattoo shop as a gruff man with a face tattoo shoved a needle through the top of my navel so I could have the same belly jewelry as Britney Spears, a hot-pink gem sitting at the center of my perfectly tanned midriff. Or perhaps it is far less interesting; not a choice at all but the result of my own DNA and upbringing, a combination of nature and nurture that had predetermined who I would be and revealed her year by year, shedding facades like a Russian nesting doll until all that was left was a small nugget of my essential self. An essential self who showers at most every other day and tells her children that toast that falls to the ground butter side *up* is still perfectly edible even though she cannot remember ever washing the kitchen floor.

Elegant Nora is no big loss, but there are other Noras who are worth my wistfulness, who I sense hanging around in my peripheral vision from time to time, urging me to look their way. Like this one: I am twenty-six years old, standing in line for the Tilt-A-Whirl at a fall festival held by a local parish. Not *my* childhood parish but the church and school that my ex-boyfriend attended. We broke up several years ago, and I spent our years apart trying on other versions of myself. Those were the years where I got a tattoo (edgy!) and did some drugs (cool!) and went to Burning Man and tried to break the mold of a Midwestern Girl Who Dated the Same Boy from High School for Nearly Ten Years. I had sex in terrible apartments with men who really didn't deserve to be inside of me, and then I moved back home to my parents' house in Minneapolis.

At night, I'd lie in bed trying not to think about what I'd done or not done with my life. My ex-boyfriend had moved back to Minneapolis to live in his parents' house and had gone to graduate school, which I only knew because we'd gotten back in touch. He'd called to ask if I wanted to go to the fair with him and his niece, a little blond girl who was born just before our breakup. It's a crisp October day in Minnesota; the exact right temperature to wear a fall jacket over a good sweater, drink hot apple cider, and step into patches of sunshine when the chill gets to you. His niece is wedged between us while the rickety metal cart tips back and forth, turning the church parking lot into a blur of colors. On the safety rail is his hand, so familiar to me, reaching over. Maybe he's just bracing himself, or maybe he's hoping that I will take it, that I will step into a different future with him and the next time we're on a shoddily constructed joyride that should really come with a personal safety waiver, it will be our own little blond girl between us, that we'll agree to be the versions of ourselves who shop at Lands' End and drive carpool and send our kids to the same schools our parents had sent us to. I don't take his hand.

I am a wife, but not his wife. A mother, but not to his children. I shop at Lands' End and I am not ashamed of it; I can highly recommend their turtlenecks for their style and durability and for a structurally sound neck that maintains its position right under your chin without strangling you. Was it that hand—the one not taken—that got me here, high as a kite in the California desert, further procrastinating my work, or some other, subtler moment that cannibalized that Nora so this one could exist? In an alternate universe, am I wearing pencil skirt suits and speaking in an even, measured voice, the sunlight hitting my unbelievable cheekbones?

Is Cate Blanchett out there, stoned, thinking about how she'll never be me?

3

Siri, Am I Losing My Mind?

The female human brain doesn't finish developing until age twenty-five, but I'm not sure mine ever really got a chance to fulfill its potential. Before the date where the brain apparently transforms from a sponge into a hardened piece of coral, I had already had at least two alcohol-induced concussions and was spending significant portions of my day online, scrolling the vast expanse of the internet, seeking out dopamine in viral videos and pictures of tiny animals balanced on human fingers. I didn't know about ginkgo biloba or omega-3s or whatever kind of dietary supplement is supposed to help keep your brain soft and absorbent; I didn't know that the buzz of alcohol was really my brain cells dying a slow and silly death. Had I known, I wouldn't have cared or changed my behavior even a smidgen. I'd have carried on being a degenerate goofball because I was having fun, and part of that fun was partaking in nights I couldn't remember, with friends I would eventually forget about entirely. Memory loss was a problem for future me, and I trusted she'd be able to deal with the consequences of my actions. That trust was entirely misplaced, because I'm not even forty yet and on a good day I'll walk into a room and ask Matthew, "What was I about to say?" as if he's a searchable database with a Bluetooth connection to my brain. I'll offer my children ten dollars to find my phone . . . only to be told that it's in my hand. More than once I've driven to a destination and found my coffee mug sitting on top of the car. Like the Maybelline commercials of yore, I'm left to wonder, "Was I born with it? Or is it early-onset dementia?" The search results are unclear, but the fear is real: I could be losing my mind.

I was seventeen when my great-aunt's dementia became evident. She'd spent over fifty years married to Billy, a Russian with big, thick fingers and a giant noggin. He'd been a boxer in his youth, and his visage maintained the confusing handsomeness of a man whose facial bones had been violently rearranged multiple times. They were an unlikely couple in an era where "Russian" was too other for an Irish Catholic family to handle, but they were married anyway. The two of them survived the Depression and World War II, and when they were unable to have children, they dedicated their lives to each other. They paid for their house on Fifty-Third and Newton in South Minneapolis with cash and designed it to be small and one level, so they could stay their entire lives. Theirs was a life of predictability; their actions set like the tiny robotic people in a fancy cuckoo clock. Each week, Billy went to the bank to get an envelope of five-dollar bills for Betty, who used that weekly allowance to get her hair set, buy their groceries, and drop a few dollars in the collection plate at weekly Mass. Billy would come home from his job at the power plant to a cold beer and a sandwich, which he ate in front of the TV until he retired and spent his days at the public golf course. Still he'd return to the same warm welcome from his wife, sometimes with my brother and me wedged next to him on the couch. They weren't our grandparents, but they sure felt like it, and when Billy died in the middle of the night, even a teenager could sense how enormous the loss was for Betty. Her life had been a response to his, and without him, she didn't know how to exist. We tried feebly to help: my father stepped in to provide her with her weekly allowance; my little brother, who was just a middle schooler, made her house his first stop after school. Betty would wait for him, with a soda instead of a can of malt liquor and cartoons instead of the local news. We showed up every day, but at night she was left on her own, alone in her little twin bed while Billy's lay empty. We thought we could create a reasonable facsimile of her former life, a bunch of clownish stand-ins for the person who'd been her constant for half a century. We didn't know that Billy's death had torn at the fabric of her reality until we saw the loose threads flapping in the wind.

One Saturday afternoon as I stood outside the Starbucks on the corner of Fifty-Third and Lyndale, I saw her unmistakable powder-blue Chevy Celebrity approach the red light. I raised my hand to hail a ride to four o'clock Mass, but she sailed right through the light and four lanes of cross traffic, completely oblivious to her great-niece, screeching tires, honking horns, and the screams of people who had narrowly avoided a multicar pileup.

It was my father who took her to the doctor, where she couldn't place the hands on a clock or tell you who the president was. Her wit and personality had covered for her in the months since Billy had died, but from this moment on, visiting with her was like walking onstage to a play that was already in progress and trying to improvise your role while the director and the star of the show changed scenes without you knowing. She began to confuse my brother for her brother, my father for her father. I became her sister Vivian, my grandmother who'd died before I was born. She slipped into these former parts of her life, and we did our best to play along and ease the pain and terror she'd feel when she slid back into a reality where all of her closest friends and family were dead, and we were just strange children telling her that it was no longer safe to heat her home with the oven.

One afternoon, when my father walked in, she began to weep like a child, clinging to him and telling him how much she had missed him. My father cradled her in his arms and ran his hands over the soft white down of her hair, soothing her like she must have done for him when he was small and scared. How frightening to know that your own brain can betray you this way, that the vessel for our sense of self is often faulty and prone to error. How awful to know that death may come for us over and over, snatching pieces of us little by little until all that is left to take is our body.

I've been informed that a key to staving off dementia is sleep, which is good news for people like Matthew. It takes approximately three minutes after lying down at night for his breath to slow to a whisper and his eyes to flutter beneath his lids. Aside from the flickering of his thick black eyelashes and a gentle snoring, he will remain in this exact position for the entire night, and for this flagrant display of unconsciousness I hate him deeply. He doesn't have a ritual or take medication; he just lies down and falls asleep. In exactly seven and a half hours, he wakes up naturally and joins our youngest children in the kitchen, feeling refreshed and energized and ready to start the day. It's revolting. While he's on a snooze cruise heading straight for REM city, I'm lying next to him hoping to fall asleep before the sun rises. My phone is in the next room, where it's been for several hours because blue light is bad and maybe that's what has been keeping me up? I have limited myself to one cup of coffee that has to be finished before eleven a.m. I have Tylenol PM and ZzzQuil on standby in my bathroom but I'm deeply afraid to take them, because what if I get addicted or I sleep too hard and pee the bed? I've meditated and breathed deeply, prayed and pleaded. My psychiatrist is stingy with her prescriptions; she's suggested that I try all the things I've been trying for decades, and because I want her to like me, I've agreed to this stupid plan. But sleep has always been an unsolvable puzzle for me, even as a child.

"Go to sleep!" my mother would cluck as she shut the door to my bedroom. "Tomorrow comes awfully early in the morning!"

And with the click of the door latch, my brain would begin counting down the minutes of rest I was missing by staying awake, calculating how unrested I would be for the next day, replaying potential scenarios that may arise the next day while I was groggy and sleep-deprived. Would Mrs. Fisher decide that it was the day for a pop spelling quiz, which she'd administer orally like a mini spelling bee? Would we be subjected to a random standardized test? My Sony bedside clock had glow-in-the-dark hands that moved audibly, ticking down to the tomorrow that would come so awfully early. In the next room, my little brother would fall asleep instantly and effortlessly, and I could hear him sleep-talking through the wall we shared.

"But Batman!" he shouted one night. "I don't even have a driveway!" Like my future husband, he would also wake up like a rebooted computer.

"Just relax," my parents would tell me, which tends to have the exact opposite effect on a person seeking relaxation. I spent most of my nights in high school talking on the phone until three or four in the morning with other insomniac teens, reading old copies of the *New Yorker* in our living room, or staring at my ceiling.

It's a strange thing to be awake while the rest of the world sleeps. But it's a strange thing to sleep, isn't it? That the entire human world has specific times and places dedicated to just . . . turning off is so adorable and hilarious to me. We as a species need this time physically and psychologically, so much so that we've designed entire rooms and pieces of furniture and supplements and devices around it. We schedule it, we accept it as a natural and nonnegotiable part of our life. Unless you're a person who can't fall asleep, in which case you're just alone in a dark house while everyone you love does the unconscious work of cleaning their brain plaque, watching a strange movie created from their thoughts and memories, and reinforcing their immune systems while you just lie there with your dirty, chaotic brain and your rapidly weakening body. Nothing stresses out a sleepless person like knowing how deeply they need sleep. I've read all the research-based tips on how to get more sleep: go to bed at the same time, stop looking at your phone, etc., etc. I've done all of this. I do all of this. And even with my phone in another room and several milligrams of CBD or THC or some newly prescribed sedatives in my system, my brain and body will refuse to turn off. Several men I know and love claim to be "microsleepers"—people who need just a few hours of rest every night—but that isn't me. I'm a macrosleeper who just can't get to sleep, and who can never get enough of it. I lust after sleep, I crave it. Once I'm finally asleep, dragging me back into consciousness is a task that requires several children, a yappy Shih Tzu, a bedside coffee delivery, and several alarms of varying tone and volume. "Ten more minutes," I'll beg my husband, who has already granted me six rounds of "ten more minutes" while getting the kids ready for school.

Sleep is important for memory, a time when, according to a TED Talk I watched, our brain takes our short-term memories and files them into long-term storage. This might explain why I've been on level 4 of Duolingo Spanish for the past year. But what is scarier than my inability to practice conversant Spanish in just ten minutes a day is the idea that I'm already losing memories, that the things I want to remember won't make it into that long-term storage. This is a nightmare for anyone, I'm sure, since our minds are where we keep our social security numbers, our childhood fears, and our essential selves. It's where I personally store lines from reality shows long out of production, what a business acquaintance's sons wore to school on their first day of school, the address of my nemesis's house and what they paid for it, and the job title of my high school classmate's husband (congrats on that promotion, Caleb). This is where I keep the knowledge that my father's former colleague voted for Bernie Sanders, that my sister-in-law's cousin hates me for my views on police violence (I personally think it's bad), that my mother's friend just bought a motorcycle, that my sister's colleague is going to India for six weeks. I could stand to lose all that, along with the parts of my brain that are storing prewritten monologues for arguments I haven't yet been invited to, and the memory of accidentally walking in on my godfather on the toilet. But I don't want to lose the way it felt as a toddler to feel the warmth of my mother's hand on my back while I tucked into her side on the sofa, or the curl of my father's lip before he told you what he really thought of "that crook Bill Clinton." What will I do without the feeling of Ralph's small fingers gently tracing my cheeks at his father's funeral, or the sound of my aunt announcing herself with a "Yoo-hoo!" as she entered a family member's home? If you could choose which parts of your brain to lose, we'd have nothing to fear. We'd be signing up to be stricken with Alzheimer's if it could be targeted to only dissolve the inconsequential or deeply cringe parts of us, the equivalent of our brain's junk drawer, filled with sticky scissors and rubber bands that have lost their elasticity and all the times we accidentally intercepted a wave meant for someone else.

Losing a few memories is not the real fear, though, is it? Our neighbor—a sensitive little girl with streams of glossy dark hair and eyes that look like they came from another dimension—was brought to hysterics by a class field trip to an historical village, the kind where groups of grade schoolers tour ancient cabins to see how the settlers lived without Wi-Fi or running water or inoculations. "They're all *dead!*" she wept to her mother at bedtime. "They're all dead, and nobody remembers them!" At nine she had realized that our memories are the only things keeping us here; a weak Velcro preventing us from being ripped from the history of time. We want to remember because we too fear existential obliteration, shudder at the thought of being lost to an endless sea of unforgettable moments long forgotten.

My family—our mother, my siblings, and all our kids and partners—took a trip to Spider Lake, Wisconsin, in June 2015. The property was a "Madge McInerny Special," meaning that our mother had booked it based on a certain kind of charm available only to her eye. That charm included cabins that were rotting and leaning precariously on the edge of a muddy lake that was unsuitable even for gazing at, electricity powered by a chain of extension cords, and a "lodge" that was a time capsule last opened in the 1960s. The weather the entire week was cold and gray, and I know this because that is what my family has told me. My brain could not—*cannot*—produce one memory of this weekend that my entire family remembers so vividly. I cannot remember our mother paddling a canoe filled with toddlers around the thick, brown water. I can't remember the dingy linens on the beds or the damp books that lined the shelves in the lodge. I insisted, when my sister-in-law Lorelei brought up the trip, that I had not been in attendance, that I must have been working, or traveling, or just not invited (it happens). But Lorelei was able to produce exact dates for the trip, which I cross-checked with my Google Photos in hopes of really sticking it to her. Instead, I was informed by cloud software that yes, I *was* at Spider Lake, Wisconsin, in June 2015. I listened as the rest of my family shared anecdotes and inside jokes from a vacation they all remembered, and I felt a sense of terror Betty must have felt every time a group of strangers walked into her home, claiming to be her family. Every shrug of my shoulders was met with another story from the trip too bad to be forgotten, my family attempting to ring a bell with no clapper. Here was the evidence that the life I loved was moth-eaten and disintegrating, one shoddy vacation at a time.

"I can't remember any of this! None of it!" I despaired, and Lorelei placed a comforting hand on my shoulder and squeezed.

"Don't worry," she sighed, "you're not missing much."

4

Holy Envy

The last time I remember seeing Eileen, I was looking up her skirt.

Soupie's was the only bar near our campus that allowed underage people (girls) into their strip-mall establishment. The bouncers would draw small, nearly imperceptible Xs on our hands to signal to the bartender that we were in no way allowed to order the five-dollar pitchers of Natural Light that had attracted us there like moths, beating against the windows in our thin, jewel-toned "going out tops" and flared, pull-on black pants in various polyblends. Nothing says "I'm here for a good time" like dressing business casual for a night out. The bouncers would use a ballpoint pen to make their marks and watch as we licked at them like kittens, rubbing the ink away easily into our highly flammable pants.

Drinking itself was not enjoyable—the first time I had a sip of beer in college I gagged, coughed, then opened my throat and poured the entire cup right down the hatch to avoid tasting it—but the warm, interior glow that resulted from drinking—the being drunk—that was one of my favorite feelings. My self-consciousness dissolved ounce by ounce, until I felt like the kind of girl who could do anything: tuck herself into a shopping cart so a cute boy could push her down a hill pretending to be E.T. and Elliott, confidently hand a bouncer an expired ID from a friend's sister, or walk up to the bar that Eileen was dancing on with her hot friends and take her hand.

The memory of that night itself is burned around the edges from time and alcohol poisoning, but I see her raven-black hair, her wide, white smile, a smattering of freckles across her pale face, and more important, every slack-jawed midwestern boy from our mid-tier private university gathered around her, their khakis tightening with every move of her hips. In that dark, crowded shithole, clouds of Camel Lights smoke hanging in the air, illuminated from above by dim fluorescent tube lights, Eileen saw me. It's me she reached out to and waved over through the crowd, me she pulled up onto the bar beside her. I was already taller than most of the boys in the room without standing on a forty-two-inch counter, but the perspective was life-changing. I was a giantess looking down on all the people who normally intimidated me so much I felt a knot of anxiety in my chest walking into the cafeteria by myself. Eileen grabbed me by the face, and we danced like extras in Britney Spears's "I'm A Slave 4 U" video, the song pumping through the speakers hanging from the corner. It's us, grinding away at each other's hips, and then the screen goes black.

That happened a lot to me in college, and in the years that followed—the night would end for my brain long before I got home (or, to someone's home)—and we'd all make a sport of trying to piece it back together the next day over omelets and Diet Coke at the cafeteria. In the harsh light of 11:45 a.m., Eileen and I looked less like sex goddesses and more like lost children. We smiled shyly at each other across the table and tried to swallow our nausea, the taste of cigarettes and light beer coating our mouths even after brushing and flossing and gargling mouthwash in the communal bathroom where someone threw up on the floor the night before.

This is not anything to brag about, but in college I was the kind of drinker who could spend all day Sunday shivering and vomiting and sipping Gatorade, literally sick from poisoning herself with cheap liquor the night before, and still make it to my eight a.m. Shakespeare class, where I sat front and center with an array of highlighters and pens to color-code my notes. Eileen was not this kind of drinker, though I didn't know that at the time. You can't tell who spends all day asleep in their dorm room skipping classes when you yourself are at your classes, but when we returned to campus after summer break, she was absent from our Power Hours, our Case Races, and our good old-fashioned Happy Hours at our favorite authentic Mexican restaurant, Don Pablo's. Her cousin told us she was taking some time off, and I felt a tug of jealousy inside me. Was that an option? Going to college felt like the lurch of a roller coaster just before it begins its terrifying descent: the previous years of my childhood were building up to this moment, following the path created by the steel dividers until it was my turn. Pulling up to my dorm room freshman year felt like the safety harness clicking into place, pushing me securely into my seat so the ride could start: freshman year, sophomore year, junior year, senior year, adulthood . . . there was no getting off the ride. College kept going until graduation day and Eileen's face, like so many others, blurred into a wash of colors as the ride went on.

Eleven years after my college graduation, I was on my first book tour, a phrase that misrepresents the actual experience, which involved me contacting any and every bookstore that would consider having an unknown first-time author for a book reading. There weren't a lot of takers, but I was lucky to get a few yeses, including one from Parnassus Books in Nashville, Tennessee, owned by the author Ann Patchett, a detail I include only because I was thrilled to be in any kind of proximity to her, however tangential. I could not hide my nervousness, standing alone in the back room hoping that literally anyone would be there to hear me read, even if they'd shown up accidentally. This is not false humility, but a reasonable reaction from a girl who was born on December 28 and very rarely had a birthday party outside of my immediate family eating cake after dinner. But there was an audience when I stepped out onto the sales floor, and when I was done talking and reading, I signed books for the few people who stayed around. I was hunched over an open book, Sharpie in hand, trying desperately to make sure I didn't mess up the spelling of my own name, when the signee asked a question.

"I think you went to college with my niece Eileen?" I looked up, and there was an older woman, definitely Eileen's aunt.

"Yes!" I said. "I loved Eileen; she was nuts! How is she?!" I was preparing to launch into the story of dancing on the bar at Soupie's but hesitated.

"She's actually—" My heart sank. Eileen was dead, and I'd almost told a story about grinding on the dearly departed to a Britney song.

"—a cloistered nun," her aunt finished, and my brain tried to decode the words I had just heard. Was this a new kind of mindfulness retreat for certain people in the know? Was I out of the loop on a new self-improvement trend?

"She's a nun?" I laughed, and her aunt beamed with the pride of a truth Catholic.

"She's a nun!" she said. "And she's never been happier. Her name is Sister Josephine Rose." Immediately she thrust a phone in front of me and there was Eileen, her pale, bespectacled face peeking out from a white-and-black habit that covered her entire body and hid her glorious crown of jet-black waves. The photo looked like it was taken from a distance with the zoom feature on a phone camera, and the result replicated the graininess and hopelessness of old disposable cameras. I was rapt with attention. There were other people to sign books for, but did any of them have this kind of information to share with me? That one of the wildest girls I'd ever met was now living in what appeared to be a haunted castle after promising her life to God? I wanted to know everything, so I wrote my email address on the inside of the book, hoping she'd reach out. And some months later, I was composing a letter to Sister Josephine Rose, the only mode of communication allowed with the outside world.

The problem with corresponding with a cloistered nun is that it's very difficult to find a topic to engage the reader. Normally when reconnecting with an old friend, I know the exact structure to take: start with a shared memory—say, dancing on a bar as underage girls—something to spark the reconnection. Once you've found solid footing, you can move into a light brag about what you've accomplished in the years since you last spoke, and then wait for them to disclose their own wins before mentally declaring a champion in the game of life. If you know their address, you can also look up their home online to see what kind of square footage and mortgage debt they're living with on a daily basis. But I just had so many questions for the woman formerly known as Eileen! What are your days like? What does your room look like? How did you end up there? And most important—is this what you want? Really? I thought about putting in a secret code, initialing random letters to spell out DO YOU NEED ME TO BUST YOU OUT? But because I wasn't sure if other people read her mail, I kept it light and breezy, telling her that in the years since we'd parted, I'd gotten married and my husband had died, but I was not a nun. Did I say breezy? I meant slightly deranged. I tried to sound Catholic enough to make it through whatever mail screener may or may not exist, and I asked if Eileen wanted to be pen pals.

Weeks went by and no reply letter arrived. Had I been flagged as a sinner, or worse—a writer?

While I waited for a reply, I did some research. Her specific monastery was lacking in a web presence, but I did find them listed on Yelp. There were no reviews. Like any spiritual organization trying to survive in modern times, there were websites dedicated to "the cloistered life," which sounded like an upcoming reality show. It's unclear who was maintaining these websites, but I learned that this specific brand (is that the right word?) of nun lived a life of "strict papal enclosure" and a life of prayer, meaning that everything they did was devoted to God. Eileen and each of her sisters were married to Christ, and there would be no lazy sister-wife jokes here. Hidden away from the world, it was their job to pray for everyone in the world. For Eileen and her sisters, the work is prayer. Sweeping the floor is a prayer, changing the sheets is a prayer. Caring for their elderly sisters at the end of their lives is a prayer.

I imagined her room as a simple rectangle with a singular window and two small twin beds, one for her and one for a roommate. I pictured them removing their heavy robes and changing into matching pajamas, saying their prayers and falling asleep until the sun rises. It feels, in my imagination, like a combination between an orphanage and a sorority. It's likely much worse. In all my digging, I found that women in her order tend to sleep on wooden planks in their full habit, waking in the middle of the night for prayer and never resting more than four hours at a time. They speak only when absolutely necessary. When people do visit, they see the sisters from behind two offset metal grilles. The vows are for life, and the sisters can only leave when they need serious medical attention. Some orders of cloistered nuns practice self-flagellation, whipping themselves with metal chains to share in the suffering of Christ.

With only these details, my mind and ego filled in the blanks and decided that my once vibrant friend was now living a quiet and deprived existence, a lonely life away from a world that missed her. I, in all my superior freedom, had taken my own vows and entered a legally binding marriage to a human man. I spend my days serving meals to children who only eat peanut butter and white bread, posting on Instagram, and creating a podcast. None of it feels like a prayer—I slipped on a pool of dog vomit recently and nearly smashed my head on our concrete floors—almost all of it feels like a relentless grind. Some nights, I too only rest for four hours at a time, though not for spiritual reasons. I lie in bed anxious that the many jobs I hold in this gig economy will all disappear, or burning with indigestion after accidentally letting a raw onion pass my lips. I imagine arriving at the monastery and demanding Eileen's freedom, her pulling off those heavy robes and shaking her dark hair loose while we peel out of the driveway and onto the open road. I'd get her a nice, soft mattress purchased with a discount code from my favorite podcast, and then what? We'd sit quietly next to each other on a couch, scrolling our phones?

Sister Josephine Rose wrote me back, eventually. The thick envelope came with one of those return address stickers you used to get in the mail for free, showing the address of her order. I opened a handwritten letter bearing the same opening line I've used in so many emails: "Sorry for the delay." She wrote that things had been busy at the monastery, and there hadn't been a lot of free time for correspondence. There was no perceptible cry for help in the handwritten pages she sent me, and she politely answered the most important questions in my initial letter: Why? And how? She told me that sometime after dropping out of our college, she ended up in a sobriety program that asked its participants to focus on a higher power. She focused so hard, the higher power called upon her to spend the rest of her life in service, to leave behind her friends and family and her given name and start anew, to leave the world behind and pray for it behind metal grilles and closed doors. She wrote that she is happy and fulfilled, that she lives with a deep sense of peace. I'm no longer sad *or* scared for her: I'm jealous.

The author Barbara Brown Taylor wrote a book called *Holy Envy*, an exploration of the jealousy one can feel when witnessing the faith of others. I've felt that holy envy a few times when I'm around a person whose faith is so strong it is the foundation their life is built on: Muslims praying at highway rest stops, Jews gathering for Passover, teenage Mormons dressed like accounting interns bravely ringing my doorbell while I hide behind the couch, afraid to hurt their feelings. I feel it now, when I imagine Eileen living her new life as Sister Josephine Rose. Maybe she just traded an addiction to alcohol for an addiction to God, but she also alchemized her own suffering into something beautiful, something holy, something private and personal and quiet.

Every beleaguered and exhausted millennial I know fantasizes about a life connected to something bigger than Wi-Fi. Meditation apps and centers abound, and mindfulness in all its forms—mindful eating, mindful parenting, mindful living, mindful working—is spoken about with full seriousness. So many of us are aching for a bit of quiet in a world that is constantly screaming at us from little rectangles in our pockets. We tell each other to practice self-care as though there are enough bubble baths to protect you from a world where you can pay fifteen thousand dollars in health insurance premiums just for the privilege of still going bankrupt with a serious diagnosis. The ride we all stepped onto as we emerged into adulthood has never stopped spinning, but Eileen has.

A prayer card printed at her monastery tumbled out of the envelope, and now it sits above my desk.

And I saw the river over which every soul must pass
to reach the Kingdom of Heaven
And the name of that river was suffering.
And I saw the boat which carries souls across the river
And the name of that boat was love.

In my reply to her, I found myself trying to match her peaceful, upbeat tone. I did not tell her that I spend the majority of my waking hours staring at some sort of screen, that my dog and I are both on antidepressants, or that I pay a stranger to listen to my problems for at least two hours a week because I don't think God has been listening to me. I did not tell her that I spend hours of my life trying to attract peace and happiness like they are songbirds and I am a pine cone covered in peanut butter and birdseed. I did not tell her that some days, the river of suffering feels like it has swept me away. I thanked her for praying for me, for us, for the whole world. *Keep it up,* I wrote, *we need it out here.*

5

The Craving

I've been an alcoholic since I was born. At least that's how my father explained it to me when I was around eight or nine years old, the age where young Catholics dress like miniature brides and grooms and take the holy sacrament of Communion, eating the body of Christ and drinking his blood from the golden chalice our parish priest kept in the tabernacle at the back of the altar. My father, I noticed, did not drink the blood of Christ from the same chalice that hundreds of other parishioners touched their lips to, whispering a quiet *Amen* to the priest's *This is the blood of Christ*, his wrinkled hands holding the cup to their waiting mouths. Instead, my father touched his fingers to the edge of the cup, head lowered, and returned to the pew.

Was my father a heathen? A heretic? Some kind of weirdo who wouldn't drink from the same cup as an old man who spent the entire service hacking into a handkerchief in the row ahead of us? No, he was something far more interesting. He was an *alcoholic*, he explained, a person who likes drinking so much that they cannot get enough of it and cannot do it anymore. My father was a handsome man with deep brown eyes shaped to portray an eternal sadness, and when I asked him why he wouldn't drink the blood of our Lord and Savior, he took me by my small shoulders and told me that whatever was in him that made him an alcoholic was in me, too; that I should watch for it. I imagined alcoholism was like the waxy black seeds that dotted our slices of summer watermelon; we'd spit them out and line them up along the edges of our paper plates because our grandfather had warned us that a swallowed watermelon seed could sprout and grow inside us, and every stomach pain would make me certain that one had slipped down my throat undetected and was taking root. At my own First Communion, I took no chances with the wine. I put my mouth to the chalice, but only until I felt the bitter-sweet liquid touch my closed lips. *Amen.*

Our mother drank glasses of red wine in jelly jars, but that was okay because she was *not* an alcoholic. Still, I eyed her warily whenever she had a glass of red with dinner. When I drank for the first time—as a junior in high school—I blacked out and woke up the next morning in my parents' backyard. I went to school on Monday with a split chin and a backpack full of shame to hear from my friends that I'd fallen off Justin Lentz's kitchen table after lip-synching to Christina Aguilera's "Come On Over Baby," and that in a few days we'd be able to pick up the photos from Walgreen's. *I will never drink again,* I thought, and I didn't. Not until the first party of college, where I did it all over again and again and again: drink, black out, shame, sobriety, repeat. My father had started drinking in high school too, but he'd kept at it for a steady thirteen years until he got sober in 1978. He told me that he'd liked the way alcohol could relieve his self-consciousness, how a beer or two would dissolve the pane of glass that separated him from the world and reveal the warm and clever person inside him. But he did not like the way a beer or two became a dozen, or the way his head pounded in the mornings, or the way his mother looked at him across the kitchen table after dragging him inside from the front porch where his friends had dumped him the night before.

My father's side of the family has been plagued by addiction for generations, though they didn't call it that. "He has the craving," they'd whisper, a euphemism for alcohol or gambling. The craving could make a person do all kinds of things they wouldn't do otherwise: they may slap their child or disappear on Christmas Day to drink in a bar downtown. They may skip off to the casino and put it all on red. The craving was corrosive not only in action but in effect: it dissolved the people we loved entirely, leaving behind yellowing, angry husks. I was warned against alcohol, but my craving was bigger than that; it was anything at all that would transport me from the discomfort of the present moment. Sometimes that's been alcohol, or the internet, but mostly my craving is craving itself, the tending of an endless hunger.

I was a skinny child, with protruding knee and elbow joints and a butt so bony my parents screamed in agony when I tried to sit on their laps. They'd marvel at how much I could eat, wrapping their thumb and pointer fingers around my biceps and asking, "Where do you put it all?" My aunt called me

Olive Oyl, and while I knew that Popeye's girlfriend wasn't a hottie, I knew that being skinny was better than the alternative. Fat, I knew, was bad. I didn't have any myself, but I heard how the grown-ups talked about my cousin, who was just six months older than me. She had "bigger bones" and "baby fat," which were things to whisper about behind her back, their voices heavy with concern. My sister Meghan was smart and beautiful . . . if only she'd lose weight. Fat was a concern, an error, something to be cured of; a *but* between you and everything good. I hated overhearing these comments, hated how they made my ears flush red in embarrassment and anger, hated how they revealed a secret side of life where even the people who love you the most could also be privately cataloging your flaws. What did they not like about me? What ways could I be improved upon? I hated even more how relieved I was to be skinny, and what a coward I was to overhear all this and say nothing in defense of the people I loved. But I *was* relieved. Skinny was good and beautiful and a secret skill I'd been born with, until it wasn't. My fellow college freshmen and I enjoyed the access to high-calorie, sugary foods without the burn of daily competitive sports, and I returned home for the summer to find that the red lifeguard suit that I'd left in my closet wouldn't go past my thighs. I was six feet tall and a size 10, healthy by any standard unless that standard was pop culture in the year 2002, where the tabloids declared Lindsay Lohan and Paris Hilton to be "scary skinny!" but still presented them as the winners of every *Who Wore It Best?* Paris insisted in every interview that she ate like a trucker—only junk food, all the time—but she looked like a sexy skeleton.

The fix for this problem was simple: twice-weekly Weight

Watchers meetings in a strip mall half a mile from my job at the public pool. Based on my goals, I was given a daily budget of points, which were calculated with an analog device made from two pieces of interlocking cardboard that provided a sliding scale of calories, fiber, and fat grams. Before eating, or thinking of eating, I would consult the sliding calculator, trying to decide if a small cup of fat-free yogurt was "worth it" or if I should save those points for half an entree at a fast casual restaurant later that evening. If you are ready to throw this book through the wall at the idea of a tall, thin woman calculating her points in hopes of *slimming down* to a 6 or a 4, I understand completely. Because years later, I still think about the other women (and yes, they were all women) who were desperate to lose thirty or forty pounds. I imagine them watching me at weigh-in every week, proudly announcing that I'd lost one pound by refusing the cake at my cousin's wedding and ordering a six-inch sub instead of a foot-long . . . and I wonder why they didn't stab me on the spot. I don't wonder why we were all there, paying money to get ourselves back under control, or why the first response to my own changing body was punishment and deprivation, or why having fat or being fat was so abhorrent to me that it needed to be remedied. This was the water we'd collectively swum in for generations, and I was simply taking my rightful place in the history of Women Losing Weight.

It didn't take long for the pounds to slide off me, for my shorts to hang loose over my hips and my ribs to show through my tan skin. Weigh-ins and points were as intoxicating as any drink, with none of the calories, which I'd started calculating with a dedication that would have made my math teachers proud. I started running before my shifts at the public pool, and swimming laps on my breaks, noting my estimated calorie burn based on what I'd read in the fitness sections of the women's magazines I'd subscribed to. Several members of my group had told me that you could "save up" points to spend later, maybe on a few bites of the lowest-calorie treat at Dairy Queen. I saved my points, but I never spent them. I went to bed hungry; I woke up hungry. Emptiness was my new friend. When I went back to school, I left the calculator behind. Something inside of me knew that my weight and my beauty needed to be effortless to be appreciated, that I had to present this version of myself as a humble surprise even to myself.

The university health center was filled with bony girls walking on treadmills, sprinting on ellipticals, riding bicycles to nowhere. Afterward, we'd light our cigarettes and walk slowly back to the dorms, buzzed on endorphins and tobacco and the feeling of having burned away more of our unruly selves, laughing at the irony of burning our lung tissue after two hours of cardio. Our bodies were objects we could mold to fit into the trendiest jeans and the smallest crop tops. It didn't take long for these college friends to be *jealous* of me. Sure, they said they were worried, but I knew the truth: it was envy. I could pull my jeans on and off without unbuttoning them. My thighs couldn't touch if I wanted them to.

When you quit drinking, you realize how much of your social life revolves around booze. When you quit eating, you realize how much of life itself revolves around food. I couldn't avoid eating *forever*, and under the watchful eye of one of my suspicious roommates, I choked down a burger and fries at the cafeteria just to prove to her I didn't have a problem.

The Craving

Panic rose in my chest at the thought of all of those abstract calories becoming fat cells, and with the shower running in the bathroom that joined our two bedrooms, I pressed the sensitive part of the back of my throat with my pointer finger and hoped I'd caught it in time. As a child I'd cry any time I vomited, but this time I felt the sweet relief of a job well done.

In the margins of my daily planner, in writing too small to be seen over my shoulder in class, I kept track of everything that passed my lips:

Mint: 5
Granola bar: 250!!!
Apple: 30

There was no goal weight, no ending point, just the satisfaction of feeling my body eat itself from the inside, the gratification of overruling my body's neediness with a militant neglect. I weighed myself every day, but the number on the scale became nearly irrelevant to me. The point was the hunger, the denial, the indulgent binge, and the repentant purge. My days and my life revolved around the craving until the craving was almost all that was left of me.

My father's parents had said nothing to him about his drinking, and my parents said nothing to me about my not eating. At least, nothing negative. Why would they be concerned that their skinny child was now a skinny adult woman? Why would they be worried that their daughter fit neatly into an ideal beauty standard that they too had been conditioned to see as good and virtuous? One of my mother's favorite stories to tell me as a child was how she used to be fat . . . until she became too busy to eat one summer and lost all the weight. She was rewarded with beauty, male attention (the most valuable kind!), and a short-lived stint as class president (she was removed from office after evidence emerged that she'd skipped class to go to a baseball game . . . that's politics, baby!).

The first step is admitting that you have a problem. The next is realizing that this problem is bigger than you. It's bigger than all of us, and a part of many of us. For decades, celebrity bodies were ranked in popular magazines and TV shows with a kind of zeal that today's culture finds abusive and abhorrent but we called prime-time TV. We watched a yearly "scholarship contest" where part of the competition included the female contestants walking the stage in bikinis and high heels, as is required in all graduate-level college courses. We watched Oprah drag a little red wagon filled with actual fat onto the stage with her to illustrate how much weight she'd lost. On the cabinet in our dining room, I keep a small black-and-white snapshot of my in-laws in the '70s. They're in their early twenties and about to be married. Jim has thick glasses and a shy smile; Shari has thick dark hair cut into a short bouffant. They're smiling in front of a house in Wisconsin, and even though the photo has no color, you can just tell that it's summer. Maybe they're on the way to a cookout, or a day on the lake. I watched recently as Shari looked at this artifact of her youth and commented sadly, "Oh . . . I always had such fat knees." The obituary for Jean Nidetch—the founder of

The Craving

Weight Watchers—states that she died at age ninety-one in 2015 . . . and that as recently as 2011, she was still at her goal weight of 142 pounds. I imagine Jean, at ninety-one, turning down slices of her own birthday cake and counting out slices of turkey for her lunch, and I think to myself . . .

How. Fucking. BORING!

How absurd! Not just in your nineties, when you're in the final countdown, but always! How absolutely boring and enraging it all is: the calorie counts and the dressing on the side and sandwiches with lettuce where the bread should be. The thigh gaps, the six-pack. How dull to sit in a group of human beings and recount for one another the contents of your week's lunch, the "tips and tricks" you used to convince yourself that you were not as hungry as your body thought it was. How bizarre to pretend that the hours and dollars we've spent to make ourselves smaller was for "health and wellness" and not aesthetics. What else could a group of twenty-five women have talked about or accomplished in that time together? What could I have learned in college had my brain and body been properly fueled? What a waste of time, potential, money, and perfectly good food!

And yet . . . I still look at old photos of myself—evidence of how deeply sick I was—and think, *Wow, she looks good.* I have never been a person for rock bottoms or see-the-light-epiphanies, and I do not have a memory of the last time I pushed up against that soft spot at the back of my throat or the last time I spent days surviving on a handful of calories. The habits changed and shifted, that germinated seed found new and more socially acceptable ways to flower: I tried juice cleanses and veganism and raw foods. I cut dairy and then gluten. I started running and exchanged calorie counting for miles and steps and various devices meant to measure my fat burning, my resting metabolic rate, my fat-burning zone. The craving has never left, I just have more ways to satisfy it. I can get ten thousand steps a day! I can sign up for a half-marathon! I can give up sugar! I can do all of this while I donate beautiful clothing that no longer fits me, telling my new body that she is bountiful and will not be contained by these inadequate garments. I'll snap at my own mother for mentioning her dress size, then privately wince at the sight of my own belly in the bathroom mirror, then wince at my wincing. To admit this—a hopelessly unfashionable addiction to the appearance of my body—is a crime in some circles. It's much more becoming to "embrace your flaws" or—even better—to not see your body's flaws at all, to firmly believe that your physical appearance is immaterial and unimportant, that your body is simply a vessel for your soul and your personality. Personally, I've found the undoing of generations of social conditioning to be slow going.

Under all addiction is pain, an unfulfilled need, a wound that needs tending to. What pain was in that black-and-white photo, that strip mall, those dorm rooms? What wounds still have not healed; and would a donut help?

6

Privacy Settings

The year I turned thirty-seven years old was the year my mother finished my baby book. It was also the year she started it, a fact I no longer hold against her. As a kid, I held a lot of grudges against my mom, which I documented aggressively in my daily journals for posterity.

Who: Margaret McInerny
What: Received the Meanest Mom Award
Why: For always—ALWAYS!!!—taking Patrick's side.
   For neglecting her second daughter and BLAMING
   HER for everything!!!

I was the third of four children, sandwiched between two brothers, the youngest of whom was *obviously* my mother's favorite, as evidenced by the journal entry above. Any attention I got was simultaneously too much and never enough, and whose fault could that be other than my mother's? Several of my friends had stay-at-home moms who welcomed us home from school with pitchers of Kool-Aid and frozen sliders fresh from the oven because they were families whose driveways were graced biweekly with a Schwan's refrigerated truck delivering all kinds of high-priced, highly processed frozen foods. My mother shopped in the bulk section of the grocery store and usually ate a dinner of Fritos dipped into cottage cheese, which she enjoyed while hunching over the kitchen counter and paging through a Lands' End catalog as her ungrateful children took turns whining over whatever meal she'd made for us after a three-hour round-trip commute to the small town where she laid out catalogs for seasonal tchotchkes for eight hours. My father, on the rare occasions when he made dinner, could poach an egg perfectly and place it on a soggy piece of toast, a meal we ate with gratitude and amazement. *Bless us, oh Lord, and these, thy gifts.* Our father was a benevolent dictator tossing us a near-literal scrap of food, but our mother was a vending machine that provided hugs and food and late nights constructing an historically accurate colonial-era diorama for history day, which she approached with the same artistry and attention to detail she brought to her paid work.

The baby book was worth the wait, because Margaret is now retired and has the time to really commit to her process and put those professional skills to personal use. The book itself is covered in a bold yellow linen, with acid-free archival-quality pages. Here, the highlights of my childhood are organized not chronologically but by theme, and annotated with her modern cursive. Unfortunate birthday parties belong together, whether that was the seventeenth birthday where my dad and I had to share a cake, or my depressing ninth birthday, which was held in a small-town Minnesota "doll hospital" where my friends and I gripped our off-brand American Girl dolls and pretended to like the dry cake served in a dusty room filled with broken doll parts. Small envelopes are occasionally pasted to the page to hold childhood ephemera like broken baby teeth (tucked into another enveloped and labeled "probably yours") or programs to the many school performances held by my strangely modern parochial school.

This book is invaluable to me. It is evidence not only of my childhood but of her motherhood. She wasn't waiting at home for us with a pitcher of Kool-Aid like Jan Mulcahy, but my mom was there in ways I doubt I am for my kids. When she left that rural photo studio, decorated for seasons that were many months away, her professional work was done. All that lay ahead was an hour-long commute back to a house where she could sink into the second shift of motherhood: packing our homemade lunches, hounding my brothers about the homework they seemed physically incapable of turning in, and making sure we were generally nourished, bathed, and ready for the day ahead. Without this book and the few boxes rotting in a storage unit somewhere, my childhood would not exist outside of my memory and the memories of my family. I'd forgotten about my favorite sweatshirt's white crewneck with a purple vector image of a stegosaurus emblazoned across the front—the word STEGOSAURUS underneath in case anyone mistake it for a triceratops—until I saw a photo of five-year-old Nora wearing it as she blew out her birthday candles. I'd forgotten about our dad's George Harrison phase in the '80s, where he let his hair grow out long and wavy.

Am I a part of the last generation to have a forgettable childhood? Not an uneventful childhood (ask me about the time my dad literally pulled the car over because my siblings and I were fighting and I was sure he was going to leave us on the side of a rural highway), but a childhood that has the ability to be forgotten, to be tossed into a dumpster or burned in a fire. A childhood that isn't backed up to the cloud, archived and available for download.

When my son Ralph was born, we were prepared. It was 2013, and my husband Aaron had just gotten out of the hospital for his second brain surgery to remove an aggressive brain tumor (glioblastoma, if you're the kind of person who needs to know). Two weeks before he stood at my feet and attempted to catch the baby I pushed out of my body (he missed), I was sitting beside his hospital bed while a catheter threaded up his femoral artery to his brain and pumped in poison designed to kill a brain tumor while hopefully not killing him.

Under the thin cotton of my Old Navy maternity T-shirt, our child pushed against his father's touch. Aaron was thirty-three; I was thirty. In the last fifteen months, he'd had two craniotomies and was starting his second round of radiation. For the first year, his chemotherapy had arrived prepackaged in orange bottles, two giant pills rattling in the bottom of each plastic container. The labels warned against the exchange of fluids, so we kept our toothbrushes in separate cups and kissed each other chastely. The baby inside me had been conceived with an act of medicine between me and a kind-eyed nurse who'd set an egg timer and wished me luck after inserting a small syringe into me, hopefully sending Aaron's thawed sperm toward the eggs that had been released with the help of a needle jabbed into my stomach the day before.

Privacy Settings

A happy, healthy family. A happy, healthy family was the prayer I mentally telegraphed out to the universe while Aaron's thin fingers rested on my belly.

"What's the baby's hashtag?" was what I said out loud.

Aaron and I were Internet People. We'd *technically* and *briefly* met in real life years before we'd connected on Twitter, but bantering online is what gave us the courage to finally meet in real life. Once we'd met, I did the customary deep creep of all his social media. I searched his Facebook for photos he'd been tagged in, and then clicked through any open albums posted by his friends to see if he showed up in the background of other photos. I used this reconnaissance to create a picture of him; he was vibrant and funny and had a social life I found intimidating and exhilarating, seeing as how most of my weekends were spent getting blackout drunk with whoever still wanted to hang out with me.

Aaron and I were in this same hospital the day we found out about his brain tumor, and we'd spent the liminal space between his CAT scan and his diagnosis staging photos for this new app called Instagram. Aaron posed in a wheelchair with a blanket over his legs, and I captioned it "my personal FDR." He posed in a bed pretending to have a seizure like the one he'd had at work before being rushed to the emergency room. It was fun and funny, because we were young and stupid. Besides, the only people who saw our photos were us and the few friends who'd decided to use the app. Everyone else was on Facebook, and once something was on Facebook, it was real. It was official.

BAD VIBES ONLY

In those few years between his diagnosis and the birth of our child, Instagram had grown exponentially. By 2013, the word "selfie" was the Oxford dictionary word of the year, and Instagram had over 152 million users who posted over 65 million photos a day. It was ubiquitous. Users didn't bat an eye when it was announced that Instagram owned every photo you posted and could use them for advertising purposes without compensating you. Who would care about something so administrative? Who could possibly make money off my filtered photos of dismal desk lunches?

At our wedding, we asked guests to post photos to Instagram with a hashtag (#purminerny). The wedding took place just two weeks after Aaron's official diagnosis of stage IV brain cancer, and the one and only time we googled his specific kind of brain cancer. The invisible countdown clock had begun. There wasn't time to wait, and there wasn't money for a traditional wedding. I ordered a red dress on the internet and kept the tags in, hoping to return it later. Aaron got coordinating Nikes. We stocked up on Costco champagne and set up a livestream for anyone who couldn't make it, which was most people on just a few weeks' notice. This was nearly a decade before COVID would make Zoom the most popular wedding venue of 2020, and the notion of putting your wedding on the internet was so novel that the *New York Times* interviewed me for a piece called "More Guests for Less (Wi-Fi Required)," where I'd apparently said, "The fact that guests were attending by the internet and computer screen didn't make it any less touching to us." The 238 guests who'd streamed our wedding were friends and family and at least one stranger who wondered why I'd chosen to wear black tights. The answer: my legs bruise easily, okay?

Later that night, lying in a hotel room bed with our friends, Aaron and I scrolled through Twitter and Instagram, double-tapping photos from the night and screenshotting the evidence that our wedding was a local trending topic on Twitter.

Ralph Purmort arrived in the world in January 2013. He had ten fingers and toes, a car seat that we didn't know how to operate, and a hashtag (#Ralphiegrams) ready to deploy any and all photos of him from that day on. I'd given up on the idea of making him a baby book before he was born. There was no need, because we'd taken the time to set up a blog for him on Tumblr.com, where every Instagram photo posted with his hashtag would create a blog post on his own personal Tumblr. We imagined this little corner of the internet collecting all the photos our friends and family snapped on holidays and weekends together, thousands of photos and memories all available for him to access anytime he wanted, forever.

There were—are—thousands of photos of Ralph on the internet. Internet acquaintances took his funniest photos and turned them into memes. I reveled in watching photos of him gain likes and comments while also pretending to be completely ambivalent about it. It feels good to be liked online; it feels just as good to watch your children be liked online. Anyone on Instagram could click #ralphiegrams and be taken to a chronological display of our child's life, could peruse any and all photos posted by a public Instagram account. But to see it on Tumblr? Oh, you need a password for that. What was that choice, if not a small whisper of the natural urge to protect our young? How quickly was it shouted down by the natural urge for validation and attention? What is the digital version of Munchausen syndrome by proxy, and how hard is it to be diagnosed and treated for it?

There are no parents on earth better than the ones who don't have children. Before I gave birth to Ralph, I swore that he would have no refined sugar, no television. He would be a free-range, screen-free child . . . while I would document the proof on *several* screens. The risk was seemingly low. I had a few dozen followers, all of whom were friends or family or friends of family. I always had a line for the kinds of photos I would share. Obviously there would be no nude photos and nothing embarrassing. I cringed at parents who posted photos of their kids smeared in their own excrement, just like I cringed writing the word "excrement" because it really is a much more upsetting word than "poop," isn't it? I wouldn't post any photos of my son that would embarrass him if I pulled them out of a photo album in front of a future partner the way meddling mothers do in rom-coms. Instead, I posted photos of him sitting beside his dad during Aaron's chemo treatments. I posted a photo of him screaming, purple-faced, after his MMR inoculation. When Aaron got sicker and entered hospice care in our home, I posted a photo of twenty-two-month-old Ralph, standing in overalls and tippy-toes peeking into his father's hospital bed.

I shared Ralph's life as if it were my own, and I defended myself to imaginary detractors with an essay about this practice in 2017. Writers don't typically choose their own head-lines, but I can't say whether or not I named the essay "My Son Is a Hashtag." I can tell you that at the time, Ralph was turning four years old and had started hissing like a cat when people who followed me on Instagram addressed him pub-licly, referencing parts of his life that he had foolishly assumed were between the two of us. I paused momentarily after each interaction, struggling with how to give him context about how a stranger would know about his imaginary brother, Gary. I paused, but I didn't stop posting. The essay was an act of passive aggression; a knee-jerk defense mechanism triggered in part by listening to the podcast *Note to Self*, where host (and truly lovely person) Manoush Zomorodi talked exten-sively about *not* posting her children online. Everything she said was logical and sensible and also deeply un-fun. If I couldn't talk about my *child* online, what could I talk about?

The essay shows evidence that my confidence in my digital parenting was fading, small blips of self-awareness between selfies with my smiling child. Social media had, I argued, replaced our diaries, our photo albums, our baby books. This was our new way to document our existence, a way to leave a mark on the world, however small and tempo-rary it be.

In 2015, I stepped off the stage at a local benefit for the American Cancer Society. I'd been asked to be a keynote speaker for their "younger demographic" at a fundraiser that I'd describe as "get fucked up to fight cancer." I'd la-bored through fourteen minutes of a thirty-minute keynote, shouting into a lavalier mic over hundreds of people angling to get their money's worth out of the open bar. Deflated and ready to disappear into anything other than this bleak reality, I opened my phone. I was tagged in several Facebook comments and tweets by friends and acquaintances absolutely thrilled to show me a BuzzFeed listicle titled "10 Pranks All Dads Need to Try Once" and the thumbnail image was my own fatherless child, drool dripping from his tiny mouth, with a set of messy eyebrows penciled onto his face. It was, in fact, not his father who had "pranked" him in this way, but me, during an afternoon with my sister while Aaron was in bed sleeping off the side effects of his chemo. I was . . . a little annoyed, but then I noticed that the listicle wasn't *just* a typical BuzzFeed listicle, but a subtle piece of branded content created by an automobile maker we'll call Nissan because that's their name. Now, I wasn't annoyed; I was pissed the heck off. The last time Ralph had been #withdad was the day his father died in our guest room. It had been just three months, and while I had just been onstage trying my best to be inspiring, in reality I was a black hole of rage and unresolved PTSD. On and on I scrolled, and more pieces floated into context.

It was Super Bowl weekend, and they were promoting a hashtag called #withdad, developed to complement their Super Bowl commercial. I imagined the marketing and advertising team that dreamed this up; the kind of team Aaron and I would have been on just a few months before. Nissan would sit at a glossy conference table with a group of mostly white men in flannel, pitching them on the virtues of "user-generated content" and "organic reach" to help "get the most bang for their Super Bowl buck" and "go viral." There would be nodding, agreement. Hundreds of thousands of dollars would likely change hands.

I tweeted to @NissanUSA on the dance floor of a crowded event venue, beneath a projected image of my dead husband; I knew that a person younger than me would get the tweet, panic, and run it up the flagpole. I spent the night drunkenly refreshing my feed . . . they hadn't replied to me.

Two nights later, I was tapping out an email, having received an anonymous tip from a Nissan insider that the communications team was aware of my tweet. I imagined a version of my former marketing self, an underpaid young woman having her fight-or-flight response triggered by my relentless tweets. This wasn't her fault; responsibility rolls uphill. My tipster provided email addresses for all four men (obviously) in charge of the campaign, and I wrote a scorcher. I signed it *best*, which we all know really means *fuck you to hell*, and I gave them a *piece of my mind about using other people's content without their express written consent.*

But legally, they didn't need my consent. The photo had been posted to a Flickr.com account my sister had forgotten was uploading all of her photos from her phone for safekeeping. Some years ago, she'd clicked a button that listed that photo as "creative commons," meaning it was legally fair game.

It did not feel fair. It did not feel good. And it didn't feel good to spew my anger lava all over a bunch of corporate men who did eventually reply with an email so generic, I wondered if it had been written by a bot. What did I want out of that interaction—an apology? A free minivan? To taste the sweet nectar of Being Right and Righteous? Because after that email, did my posting habits about my son change? No, they did not. His childhood continued to unfold in the feeds of countless strangers, as my own Instagram following grew from eighteen thousand to fifty thousand to over one hundred thousand.

I wrote, two years later in that *Today's Parent* essay, that I reserved the right to change my mind. And as minds tend to do, mine has changed. Ralph's Tumblr is now defunct and deactivated. #Ralphiegrams has been relinquished to the general public, who use it mostly to tag photos of their dogs. Ralph *is* a great name for a dog.

What was the Big Moment that made me pull him back from the internet? I couldn't tell you, because there wasn't one. There were hundreds of little moments, like him holding his hand up like a badgered celebrity, shouting, "No photos!" as I picked him up on his first day of preschool, or leaning in to the camera for a selfie with me and then asking ten minutes later, "How many people like it?" It was his impression of me at age four when he found an old iPhone in his toy bin and picked it up.

"Hold on, I'm on Instagwam," he said in his little elfin voice. There was the nagging feeling that instead of documenting his childhood—gathering the ephemera together in one place—I was displaying it, defining it, robbing him of the chance to tell his own story on his own terms. Ralph was a character in my own one-woman show, where I played the role of mother. I was not a mom influencer—nobody was coming to my feed to learn how to pack a bento box lunch or for outfit inspiration—but he was the person I shared my life with, the person my life revolved around. Our family was a two-person unit. I no longer had a partner to bore with the minutiae of my day, nobody to lock eyes with as our child attempted to stab a mac-and-cheese noodle with his dull plastic fork, no real-time witness to the miracle of a growing child. Along with dopamine and validation, Instagram stepped into the role of witness for Ralph's and my life. Every post was a call for attention, every like and comment a response: you are here, we see you.

When I remarried and Ralph became a youngest child, the simplicity of sharing his life online was more complicated. Not posting the children I acquired by marrying Matthew felt like I was omitting them from our life. It felt like that for them, too. They were old enough to google me, and old enough to ask why I hadn't posted photos of them. The answer was tangly: Did they want me to? Did their father? Their mother? A new awareness of boundaries with them made me question why I felt so free with Ralph's image. When I gave birth to my youngest child and Ralph became a middle kid, I created a new and only slightly rational boundary: I'd withhold our baby's real name and I'd only post photos of Ralph and the older kids with their consent. For a while that worked to assuage my guilt. "They see everything that's posted before I put it up," I said to myself, as if a person who still hadn't learned to define his left and right feet could possibly understand the terms and conditions of an app that I myself had blindly accepted.

One night I spent hours going through my feed, deleting or archiving every photo with his face in it. "I'm not posting photos of the kids anymore," I told Matthew. The declaration didn't seem to hold any gravity with him, which disappointed me. Didn't he see how morally correct I was? How I could see the error of my ways and was now superior to so many other mothers? He did not.

I rarely take photos of any of the children anymore, not because I'm *more present* and *living in the moment* or *limiting my screen time*, but because without the dopamine reward of likes, the stimulus has lost its magnetism. When I do take photos, I'm reminded not only what a crappy photographer I am but that I'm also just like my mother; these photos won't sit in envelopes inside boxes in a basement for decades, they'll sit in the cloud until they're randomly deleted. And if my generation is ever able to retire, Ralph and the others are going to have to be satisfied with the cardboard box in my closet filled with his drawings and birthday cards and undistributed school photos.

Who is Ralph? That's for him to discover and define. But I can say with certainty that he is definitely not a hashtag.

7

Who Would You Be?

Choosing a therapist is like dating; it's supposed to be perfectly acceptable to shop around, to ask questions and figure out if it's a mutual fit before you move forward into a relationship. But I never dated that way; I either settled for whoever liked me or, in the case of both my marriages, tripped and fell right into the exact right match. Same for therapy. I've ghosted plenty of men and therapists after awkward hours spent across from each other hoping for a spark of energy, and I've fallen into deep and rewarding relationships that have helped me to better understand myself. I've met loves and therapists through friends and online. The website for *Psychology Today* functions just like Match.com, letting you sort by geographic range, specialties, and accepted insurance. For the shallower among us, you can just choose according to headshots, the way nature intended.

People will tell you that when it comes to therapists, you might need to date around and find the right fit, but whenever I've needed therapy, it's been just that: a need. There's no time for shopping around when you're desperate, and by the middle of 2020, I was as desperate for a therapist as I had been for a boyfriend in my early twenties. I googled and filled out online forms and left voicemails, and the first person to get back to me was a kind-faced and credentialed man named Allen, who could meet with me that week. He fit all my criteria for dating and therapy: he was alive and available.

Given that we were a few months away from vaccinations for COVID-19, I was delighted to know that he was willing to meet in-person as long as we stayed on opposite sides of his office and wore masks. I've always thought it would be much more efficient to start a relationship with a therapist by saying, "Could you just google me and tell me your first impressions?" But that's "unethical" and it's a part of their job to actually get to know you, which means that you have to start every therapeutic relationship the same way you start a first date: by giving enough information to be considered honest and interesting without being overwhelming. I wasn't sure if I should start right at the beginning and tell him how I was born fourteen days past my due date and in respiratory distress—which obviously explains why I cannot be on time and why I hate doing cardio—or if I should just skip to the headlines, like when my dad and my husband died right after I had a miscarriage. Should I start with where I am now and work backward? I spend a lot of my work life interviewing other people, and it was hard to fight the urge to lead the conversation and steer it back to him, but Allen is a professional, and he asked me, simply, "What brings you in today?"

"Well," I said, staring at the space above his head, "I think it's mostly that I hate myself and everything about me? My life is objectively good, but nothing makes me happy, and everything is either disappointing or overwhelming." I spent the next forty-eight minutes crying until my face mask was soaking wet.

The next week, I arrived with some evidence to support my thesis that I'm a Bad Person: I'm impatient with my children and I sometimes speak sharply to people I care about. Compliments slide right off me and are evidence that the complimenter has no idea what they're talking about. When my youngest tells me I'm the "best mom ever," I know it's only because he doesn't know that many moms, and if he did, he'd know I don't play nearly enough with him.

A key part of being a therapist is that the sessions are about your clients, not you. Therapists—good ones, at least—are skilled at giving as little of themselves to you as possible. You won't hear what careless words their mothers said to them as a child that forever wounded them; you won't know where they go to the gym or what they want for their birthday. You won't even know they *have* a birthday. They're meant to be a nearly anonymous and yet deeply intimate figure in your life, a wise person who can listen and reflect back what you told them with a glimmer of insight. And during our third session, that's what Allen did.

"I've noticed that you don't seem to have a lot of compassion for yourself," he said gently.

Compassion? For myself? Why would I give myself compassion? I've met myself, and I'm a dumb bitch who was at least a sophomore in college when she realized that engineering majors were not in school to learn how to drive trains. Why would I spend my time treating myself with the tenderness I extended to other people? What a waste of time when after all, we only have twenty-four hours in a day to produce and create and fill out forms and eat and sleep and parent and make sure that the dog has been walked before she pees on the new dining room rug. When would I possibly have time to have compassion for myself when there are so many things to *do*?

Aaron was sickeningly mentally healthy, even when he was deeply sick with brain cancer. Sure, he experienced the full range of human emotions, but he experienced them all lightly and temporarily. For me, every feeling has always been big and intense and the only feeling I will ever have. You know how some people go through something and then learn from it? Not me; I have immediate emotional amnesia and everything I feel is for the first time and will certainly be permanent.

Aaron and I both worked in advertising when we met, and the highs and lows of client work were hell for me. A rejection of my ideas was proof that I was stupid, and luckily many of my colleagues were men who didn't think any ideas but their own had any merit. I spent every workday walking on a thin tightrope of self-esteem, and by the time I left at seven or eight at night, I had plummeted into the depths of despair. Across town, Aaron spent his days working as a graphic designer and art director at a rival agency. He took feedback graciously, even when it was annoying. Most of us in the industry dreaded client feedback, how they'd always have *input* for the representation of the brand for which they were responsible. Could the logo be bigger? The tagline be incorporated into the copy? Most of us would cringe, but Aaron would smile amiably and get back to work. "It's not *my* website," he'd say. "What do I care if they want it to be different?" Meanwhile, the rest of us would spend at least a half hour after client calls recapping all the ways our client was wrong about what they wanted, then go home and stew over it some more.

During the cotton-candy days of our early courtship, when everything was sweet and fluffy, I tried to warn him about me.

"I just get really sad sometimes," I minimized, "ya know?" He did not know.

"Just, sometimes I think nothing matters and like, why try?"

He looked at me blankly before his eyes softened with pity. "That sounds horrible," he whispered back, kissing the top of my head and then shaking it gently. "Stop doing that, brain!"

I've been telling my idiot brain to stop it for decades now, and she just won't *listen*, not even to professionals. But there are moments after a particularly good night's sleep or a conversation with a friend or a therapy session, where the clouds in my mind part enough for me to think, *Wait, I'm fine!* I don't need to explore the deeper recesses of my being in search of a cure for who I am! With my mind's eye set to Panorama, my existence is placed in a wide and blurry context, and for at least a few minutes I am *good*. So good that I'd want to throw open the windows and shout about my fineness to the world, but our windows are old and many of them are painted shut, so by the time I'd get the window to creak open, the moment would pass, replaced with a constant, low-grade panic running through my veins where the blood ought to be. This is a frenetic energy that has turned me into the kind of magician whose one trick is pulling the tablecloth out from under a full dining set. Someday, I know, it will all clatter to the ground in a heap. Someday, we will not be able to *do*. Someday is probably not even that far away. I was served an ad that proudly stated: "This ad was written by AI," so robots are coming even for the jobs we told ourselves could only be performed by a sentient being with a working knowledge of a QWERTY keyboard. Someday my own brain may turn to mush, my hands may not be able to type, my voice may not be one anyone wants to listen to. Even motherhood is a basket too small to hold all our eggs. Our children—God willing—will grow up and move out, will establish their own lives and families, our importance in their lives shrinking and shifting so that we are no longer the sun but some outer planet that upon further inspection actually may just be a defunct satellite stuck in their orbit.

It's that fear—that I'm really just space junk—that has seemed to drive every version of myself. I've spent years collecting accomplishments and taking little to no joy or satisfaction in any of them, constantly thirsting like Tantalus rooted in his pool of water. I said something like this to Allen, and I was ready for him to lean back in his comfy chair and say, "Wow, what a brilliant insight; I should write that down."

"I have a question for you," he said in his calm, measured way instead. "If you didn't do *any* of these things—if tomorrow you woke up and you didn't have any of these jobs or titles—who would you be?"

I paused, my eyes searching the drop-tile ceiling.

"I'd probably go back to school and get a master's degree, I guess? I can't really go back to advertising since I've burned all those bridges, but I might be able to pick up a little free-lance copywriting—"

"No," Allen interrupted gently, "I didn't ask what you would *do*, I asked who you would be."

I stared at him blankly. "Like I said, I'd *probably* go back to school."

Silence.

"Who would you *be*?" he asked again, as if the answer were obvious. "Who would *you* be?"

What a strange and inappropriate question! It reminds me of a think piece from a few years back that suggested new questions to stand in for "What do you do?" And while the piece was earnest and well-written, I also found it comically absurd to imagine meeting a stranger at a dinner party and asking, "What makes you feel alive?"

"Oh," they may reply, "running a yellow light?" Or maybe "the feeling of crushing a baby bird in my hand." See? It's just too risky. I'd rather know where you spend your weekdays. We've been fielding the question "What do you want to be when you grow up?" since we were old enough to speak. That the *what* is a job is implied; no child instinctively says, "I think I'll be interesting and generous!" At four years old, my youngest child told us that he was going to be a "DNA scientist," and when he heard the grown-ups cooing over what a good idea that would be (sounds lucrative!), you could see the neural pathways forming in his little brain. Grown-ups ask kids what they want to be when they grow up, and they ask other grown-ups what they do, and around and around we go, defining ourselves and one another. I'm floored by Allen's question because I've never been asked such a thing, and the question itself feels like the kind of brainteasers whose answers are obvious: *The doctor was a woman! You don't bury survivors of a plane crash!* I let the silence fill the space between us.

"You'd be *you*, Nora," he said with a gentle smile, and my confusion was in no way lessened.

"I'd be who?"

"You. You're *you*. No matter what you do or don't do. You're *you*."

His face told me that this was a good thing, but my mind knew better.

I'm *me*?

Oh.

How sad.

8

Strongest Girl in the World

I consider myself lucky to have grown up before the age of helicopter parenting, snowplow parenting, or really any kind of parenting at all. In December 1982, my mother and father took me home from the city hospital in something called a "car seat," a single piece of molded plastic that the hospital was handing out to new parents. It was secured by the shoulder seat belt and placed in the back seat of their Toyota Tercel next to my mom's purse and whatever detritus my older siblings had left behind. My sister Meghan is eight years older than me, and when I was nine months old, I took a ride down the front stairs of our house in my walker while she was supposed to be babysitting me. That's how my parents told the story, that my nine-year-old sister was asleep at the wheel, totally irresponsible and completely at fault for the fact that I'd eaten concrete and been found like a turtle on its back by our elderly Polish neighbor. When I got a bit older, I routinely rode my bike with the wind whipping through my vulnerable, helmet-less hair and spent time with various neighborhood

71

children playing by active railroad tracks. When my local library was under construction the summer before fifth grade, my mom left me at home with a quarter and verbal instructions for taking the city bus to the closest library with a decent kids' section.

I didn't just grow up before the age of parenting as a verb, I grew up in an age with blessedly little for entertainment. Our children will never understand the sorrow of *missing your favorite TV show* or scouring the video rental place for a movie that is both available and of interest to you and your three siblings. New releases were never our game—they were more expensive, and hardy ever available. We'd rent The Three Stooges or The Little Rascals, anything that allowed our father to relive his favorite childhood memories, which were mostly pratfalls, sight gags, and classic racism and misogyny. But our favorite rentals were the stories of Pippi Longstocking, available in Technicolor and dubbed from the original Swedish. Pippi is a true hero for young children. She isn't orphaned but her mother is dead, her father is a sea captain, and she lives in a ramshackle house called Villa Villekulla with a talking horse and a cast of animal friends. Pippi is the hero of her own story, the Strongest Girl in the World, dressed in mismatched socks and crooked braids in her blazing red hair. She's the muse for the straightlaced kids next door, who are burdened with parents and matching clothes and the expectations of a world where children have to do horrible things like eat balanced meals and go to school. We'd finish a Pippi VHS in my cousins' basement and head directly outside, where we'd climb the massive pine in their backyard or set up a home for ourselves behind their front hedges, strategizing about how we could live on our own without their parents noticing the cheese slices we'd swiped from their fridge.

But the cabin was truly where we lived our Pippi dreams. Our grandparents' cabin was not a *lake home* or a *cottage*, it was not a place with multiple bedrooms and bathrooms, a palace on a pristine waterfront where they went to escape the hustle and bustle of the city while living in luxury. This was a pile of logs situated on a steep incline above a lake so deep and icy that the water appeared to be black. They'd inherited it from my grandfather's uncle, a Catholic priest who had inherited it from his parents and used it as an ascetic spiritual retreat. When my grandparents retired, they "modernized" the cabin with running water (fancy!) and a small powder room, and excavated a small, dank basement accessible only by the outside. The basement held a tin shower stall with three minutes' worth of hot water, and so when the temperature was tolerable, my grandparents bathed in the lake, using homemade soaps that wouldn't disturb the ecosystem.

The trip to the cabin was three long hours by car, an absolute eternity for all of us, especially since our parents were dedicated to completing the drive with no stops. "You better empty that bladder before we go, because we aren't gonna stop!" they'd remind us as we loaded into hot sedans. "It's an awful long drive when you gotta pee." This was also before children were urged or encouraged to drink water, and dehydration was considered a travel necessity. The drive itself was hell, but at the other end was even more freedom than we experienced at home. Our mothers would unpack the coolers they'd lugged up with all the food we'd need for the coming weeks, and we'd claim our beds and then run outside and down the steep incline to the lake.

BAD VIBES ONLY

The time we spent up north was both dreamy and fraught. The cousins and our parents all stayed next door in the un-insulated, one-room structure called Walter's, named for the reclusive man who had lived (and died) there many decades earlier. Our moms—sisters—would each drive the three-plus hours from the city up to their parents' cabin for long stretches without our dads, who either were working or didn't think it was a vacation to spend a full week with four to seven children in a one-room cabin. The cabin had few rules:

1. No kids inside during the day, unless you have to poop. Otherwise, pee in the lake or the forest like a normal person.
2. Should you be allowed inside the cabin and want to exit, do not allow the screen door to slam. Instead, guide it to a secure and near-silent closing, or you will immediately lose cabin access.
3. Take all you want, but eat all you take. There is no reason not to maintain good standing in the Clean Plate Club.

We slept in used military cots thrifted from auctions and estate sales, piled with quilts sewn by my grandmother and her mother. We drank icy, iron-flavored well water we pumped from the front yard and ate all our meals at the picnic tables our grandfather had placed between his cabin and ours.

Kids were allowed in our *grandparents'* cabin by invitation only. Occasionally, Grandpa would unlock the screen door and call for one or two of us to enter their small, sweet-smelling home. He'd pan-fry some sunfish in butter, or hand us a Brach's caramel or, if we were exceptionally lucky, open a glass bottle of Coca-Cola and split it into small antique glasses for us to savor before reopening the door and gently pushing us back out into the woods.

The cabin was a fifteen-minute drive from the nearest town, an unincorporated collection of small, low buildings, most of which pulled double duty. There was a bait shop/general store, a laundromat/post office, and a gift shop/ice cream parlor. Going "into town" for ice cream was a treat and a rarity, and we became fixated on the trip into town as soon as we settled into the cabin. Our few dollars of spending money were burning holes in our pockets, and our brains were on fire with the consumerist possibilities: I'd long ago given up hope that I'd ever find a small license plate printed with my name, but the gift shop *did* sell Troll dolls and novelty pens and penny candy that—go figure—cost five cents apiece. But our mothers, mothers who rarely swam *with* us and rarely took the winding switchback footpath all the way down to the water, always swore that they had *finally* just gotten to sit down, always had a reason not to take us for ice cream: it was too hot, it was too cold, they were *tired*. They parked their butts on the Adirondack chairs on my grandparents' deck with copies of the *New Yorker* and plates of cheese and crackers and enjoyed their time together. By three p.m., they were having gin and tonics or glasses of wine, and we were hiking back up the trail from the water, sunburned, thirsty, and bubbling with the adrenaline of the temporarily feral. We were not tired. We were hungry (for ice cream, not regular *food*), and we were largely unsupervised for most of the day.

And maybe that's why, at ages nine and ten, my cousin Fuzz and I ended up on our first unsupervised maritime voyage.

The fated canoe had spent most of its life lodged on the shore, covered in dead leaves and crawling with daddy long-legs. Fuzz grabbed fishing poles and some long-expired bait from our grandpa's tackle box, I grabbed the faded orange life jackets that hung from nails on the pine trees by the dock, and we pushed off on our journey. Our knowledge of geography was rather limited, given that we were children. Town was just a few minutes away! By car and road. By water it was closer to three miles away. That's far for an adult of reasonable physical fitness, we were children. Weak little children, alone on the open water, feeling the thrill of independence. Fuzz sat in the front of the canoe, because she was smaller than me and it felt like the safest place. Her white-blond hair glowed in the sun, and we drifted in circles, trying to figure out how to steer using the ancient wooden paddles, peeling and warped from decades in the sun. Feeling ever more adventurous, Fuzz and I stopped twenty-five yards off the dock, right in the middle of the lake and in the path of any oncoming speedboat, and cast a few lines, suspicious that our mothers might develop the ability to see through trees from the deck above. Fishing was an unambiguously innocent endeavor, much more defensible than our experiment of briefly going AWOL. When we were sure nobody had noticed us, we paddled a little farther, the canoe zigzagging slowly through the dark waters. "Watch out for the lily pads!" we shouted at each other, convinced that these patches were filled with vicious, girl-eating fish and snapping turtles. We were offshore without permission, and so far nobody had noticed. We paddled a little farther, and then a little more. We were officially around the bend and out of the line of vision for anyone who might walk down to the dock and look for us. We were *free*.

Fuzz and I are both middle children, mercurial and fussy and highly emotional, the kind of kids who were always told to "calm down" and "stop stomping your foot or Rumpelstiltskin will come for you." We were adversaries as often as we were allies, since she had the unfortunate position of having a cool older sister whose approval I was constantly seeking. But out here, we were undoubtedly on the same team. Without our siblings and our parents and the familial roles that had defined us, we were strong and independent, forged in the image of Pippi but with straight blond hair worn too short to braid. Like Pippi, we had money of our own and a seaworthy vessel and no adults to interfere. Out here on the open water, we could sing the Pippi Longstocking theme song at the top of our lungs if we wanted to, and we did, because maritime law says you can sing whatever you please when you're on the run in your family's canoe. The rope swing we'd heard about—the one our older cousins swam to—came into view. We'd been told we were too young, that it was too dangerous. But that was *then*, when we'd been at the mercy of authority. Now *we* were in charge, so we paddled over and climbed up the rough boards hammered into a lakeside tree and took turns flying through the summer air, the rope burning against our bare skin as we tumbled awkwardly into the freezing lake water. We emerged sunny and sputtering and sore, eager to try it again.

We knew that town was basically . . . to the left? But we didn't know that our lake wasn't a circle but a long, crooked line that wound back and forth. We could swear that town was just around every bend, but all that awaited us after every turn was more shoreline, more water, more adults passing two unsupervised children in a canoe and asking absolutely no questions, just holding up their hands in the universal sign for "We're on vacation, please don't ask me for anything." The blazing summer sun beat down on our bare heads, our hands cramped around the rough paddles, and we had already sung through *The Lion King* soundtrack several times. We were just about losing hope when we saw it: a few brown and weather-beaten buildings on the shoreline, and the small overpass we'd only ever seen from the back seat of our mothers' cars.

We stumbled to the shore with the desperation of men who have been searching the desert for an oasis, abandoning our canoe on the beach and crossing the street without bothering to look both ways. It's always more fun to spend money when the money isn't yours, and the piles of change we'd brought with us didn't have the same potential in the harsh fluorescent lights of the gift shop. There would be no Troll doll or novelty pens today. We counted out our pennies to pay for the necessities: two ice cream cones, a bag of pork rinds, and two bottles of root beer, which we chugged immediately in unwitting preparation for our college years. We'd chosen bubble gum–flavored ice cream, a strategic choice because the pink ice cream itself not only tasted like bubble gum but also contained little pieces of candy-coated gum, a treat within a treat. We took great care to extricate each piece of gum from our cone and store it in the pocket of our cutoffs for later, emergency sustenance held at the ready for our journey home.

We didn't know how long it had taken us to get to town,

because neither of us owned a watch or had bothered to consult a clock before leaving, but the sun was sitting a bit lower in the sky, casting long, cold shadows over the lake. A small pang started in my stomach and spread toward my chest: our siblings would have reported us missing by now, and our mothers would be looking for us. Back when my mother was a child, a freak tornado had ripped across the lake and into a summer camp. My grandmother had told us that two children died, that volunteers had come from around the country to dive into these deep, dark waters to find the bodies. "It was horrible," my grandmother would say. "Can you even imagine?" Well yes, I *could* imagine. I *did* imagine. I imagined it right now, standing on the public dock, tossing the rest of the pork rinds into the water for the waiting fish. We had to get back to our mothers. The adventure had to end.

The trip home did not have the joy or magic of the trip out. The lactic acid had already settled in our spindly little arms, and our brains didn't have the luxury of wondering how far it was to get home, because we already knew: it was far, and we were tired. "Maybe someone will feel bad for us and tow us home," Fuzz said hopefully, and we did our best to put on long faces for the speedboats, who ripped by us without a glance, their wakes pushing us into the dreaded lily pads. Fuzz swore she saw a snapping turtle, and the two of us screamed in terror at the thought of those ancient lake monsters upturning our boat to eat us *and* the soggy chewing gum in our pockets. We were losing steam, and hope.

"Hey," said Fuzz, standing up and wiggling out of her shorts, "I have an idea."

Our arms were beat, there was no denying it, but we

still had fresh legs. And as competitive swimmers, they were strong and meaty. Fuzz's idea was simple but genius: we'd *push* the canoe home. We each popped a few pieces of damp bubble gum into our mouths to fortify us for the journey ahead. Fuzz took the rope at the stern of the canoe, I kept an arm at the keel, and together we frog-kicked along, shouting back and forth that yes, this was much easier and yeah, I think it's going faster, too. Happy hour must have started, because the traffic on the lake started to pick up with more and more grown-ups tootling by, completely unconcerned to see two children treading water beside an empty canoe. Even this pathetic display did not entice a single adult observer to intervene. We could have been at that for hours, or minutes, but eventually the idea of a snapping turtle removing our toes, or of brushing against one of the unfound bodies of the tornado victims was too much, and we gave in, scrambling into the empty canoe, thrashing and kicking and eventually flopping onto the hot aluminum in frustration and relief.

We'd had the foresight to fill our root beer bottles with iron-tinged well water while we were in town, but by now both of them rolled from side to side on the floor of the canoe, empty, while we tried to get back into paddling position. The knowledge that we were literally out of our depth sat between us in the canoe, where it would have been useful to have a cooler or even some flares. But Pippi Longstocking wasn't going to give up just because her arms and legs were a little bit tired and her skin felt like it was going to burn off. The Pippi we knew didn't *get* tired; she could lift a horse! So we paddled on, softly singing our rendition of the Pippi Longstocking theme song and hoping that our dock would appear soon.

We occasionally took breaks to relieve our blistered palms in the cool lake water, wondering how much trouble we'd be in when we finally docked. Our grandpa would lose it for sure; there was no way we'd be invited into the cabin for buttered sunfish now. Our moms would struggle to balance their relief with their rage. They'd clutch our faces between their hands, hold us close and whisper into our hair, "Don't you ever do that again." Maybe they'd had time, in the past eight hours, to self-reflect. The mother in *Home Alone* realized after leaving her problem-child son behind and flying all the way to France without him that *she* was the problem. Maybe my mother would realize that, too. Maybe she'd beg for my forgiveness, apologize for all the times she'd sided with my little brother Patrick. Oh, Paddy! He was so tender! I made a note to be extra kind to him. He would definitely cry when he saw me, the sister who he had spent the day assuming was either dead or abducted.

There was nobody waiting at the dock when we returned. We quietly pulled the canoe to shore and replaced the fishing poles and the life jackets and the tackle, heeding our grandfather's favorite saying, "A place for everything and everything in its place." The solid earth under our sea legs was a relief, but we both took our time walking up the trail to the cabin. There were no sirens, no commotion, just the familiar sounds of our mothers and grandparents in place in their Adirondack chairs, the smell of sweet corn leading us back toward the cabin. Our brothers and sisters were lining up for dinner when we stepped up onto the porch, waiting to be noticed and admonished, worshipped or grounded forever. But our siblings asked no questions, and our mothers made no comments. We'd had the biggest adventure of our young lives, had been absent for hours, and *nobody had even noticed we were gone*.

The likelihood of Fuzz and Nora's Okay Adventure happening in the twenty-first century is nearly impossible: today's grown-ups would definitely cut the engines and come to the rescue of two children *pushing a canoe*. They'd then contact the cops, the local news, their social media influencers and mommy bloggers of choice, and make sure that our mothers were properly shamed, their faces spread across the internet because mothers in this century are expected to know exactly where their kids are at all times, because their kids are always with them or under the watchful eye of another legally liable adult. The adventures are structured and supervised, and I'm not saying this is *bad*, but it's hard not to look at my children, who are currently sitting side by side on the couch watching YouTube videos of *other children playing video games*, and not feel a teensy bit bad for them.

What stories will they have to share about their childhood when they've always had an adult hovering at the periphery of their vision, cautioning them to watch their head or slow down or take smaller bites? Who is *their* Pippi Longstocking, filling them with the belief that they too could live a life of joyful independence, of tossing large mammals in the air, of wearing mismatched socks and living in a dilapidated mansion populated with barnyard animals? If my soft-handed little gamers had the opportunity to hijack a canoe in pursuit of ice cream and independence, would they take it? And how far would they get before they turned around to find Wi-Fi?

9

Reunion

What I know about high school reunions is that they are supposed to make you vibrate with anxiety over the way you'll be perceived by the people whose perceptions of you were central to building your own sense of self during the rocky years of your adolescence. I know this mostly from the movie *Romy and Michele's High School Reunion*—a movie I watched before I'd even attended high school—starring Academy Award–winner Mira Sorvino and Emmy Award–winner Lisa Kudrow as two former nerds turned hot airheads who return to their ten-year high school reunion ready to impress their former classmates. The problem, of course, is that nothing they've done is particularly impressive. They live in crappy apartments, work crappy jobs, and have yet to hit any of the "real" milestones of adulthood like marriage or motherhood. So they do the only thing that makes sense: put on some lady suits, borrow a convertible, and stroll into the reunion claiming to have invented Post-its. This movie came out when I was in middle school, when Erin and Cara and I spent our weekends producing original soap operas in Erin's partially finished basement or having "worm fights" where we'd crawl headfirst into zipped sleeping bags and wrestle. The movie was rated R, but Erin's mother had once mistaken *The Hand That Rocks the Cradle* as a children's film, so slipping it by her at Mister Movies was hardly a challenge. We understood exactly zero of the sex jokes, but we understood the moral of the story, which was that your high school crush will end up a loser, the nerds will end up successful, and anyone you need to try to impress is not worth impressing. It was this wisdom, I believe, that got me through the rougher patches of high school. That it would pass, that there would be more.

I either missed my ten-year reunion or wasn't invited. Either way, I found out about it while it was in progress less than a mile from where I was at the time, which was standing at a party looking at my phone. "What the fuck?" I'd said. "My high school reunion is tonight?" I shoved my phone toward Aaron as if he'd be able to recognize any of the people on the tiny screen of my iPhone 4s. "Hm," he'd said, raising his eyebrows, "looks like *someone* wasn't invited!" He was joking, and I laughed, but just down the street, the DeLaSalle High School class of 2001 was reconvening without me. Had I been intentionally excluded? Why? And how! We all had Facebook, which is how I knew that Margaret was a dentist who married a man with her same last name, that Andy was in the process of becoming a doctor, that Alan had ended up in the NBA . . . and I'm sure they all knew that I . . . well, I hadn't done much, I guess. I didn't talk about my job online because how do you tell people that you spent weeks put-

Reunion

ting together a social media strategy for a brand of chicken when most people don't even know that there *are* brands of chicken? How do you tell people you're not married and your father is *worried* because when he was your age, he had two kids and a mortgage and you, in his words, "have credit card debt and split ends"?

Oh well, I thought, *there's always the twenty-year!*

Ten years seemed like a lifetime away, more than enough time to become myself, or at least a version of me I'd be proud to show people. Maybe I'd be married by then, or have a career. Maybe, in another decade, I'd like myself.

My high school is more than just *my* high school. It's a Minneapolis and McInerny family landmark, established over one hundred years ago smack dab in the middle of the Mississippi on Nicollet Island, built in the 1900s by the Christian Brothers to bring education to all (white) boys, regardless of income. And while private school conjures up images of fanciness, the location of this school was a part of the city's skid row for most of its existence. When my grandfather attended this school, downtown Minneapolis had horse-drawn carriages and streetcars. He was kicked out two weeks into his freshman year after one of the teachers looked out the classroom window after school and spotted Austin Clifford McInerny smoking a cigarette while walking across the Washington Bridge. Decades later, my father, Stephen, would enroll, and see a transient shot in the stomach outside a flophouse across from the freshman building. Two years later, Dad would face expulsion for coming to class dead drunk,

85

but then negotiate with the principal for a lighter sentence of joining the cheer squad at an all-boys high school where the homophobia and misogyny were strong enough for that to be nearly equivalent to an expulsion. Twenty-five years after *that*, when the school had begun to enroll women and Black and brown people, my brother and sister would enroll and call each other in sick from the pay phone in the lobby. By the time I got there—a decade later—we had school uniforms and at least one school bus and the flophouse where my dad saw a murder was now a town house worth hundreds of thousands of dollars and our basketball and football teams were winning state championships.

My graduating class was filled with kids whose parents had gone to high school with my parents, aunts or uncles, whose own family histories intersected with parts of mine.

"Mullen . . ." my dad said upon meeting a classmate of mine. "Any chance you're related to Greg Mullen?"

Fifteen years after I graduated, our son handed his application to the same admissions manager who had reviewed my application in 1998. On the tour, I spotted a slightly upgraded version of my own high school, greeting some of the same teachers who had given me detention for having my shirt untucked. Over the years, he's worn the same uniform shirts I'd worn, walked the same halls, attended (or didn't) the same dances. Every time I stepped on campus to drop off his forgotten lunch or come to a soccer game, I felt the flickering ghosts of everyone I'd been while I was a student here, an emotional residue that remained in the hallways and the bathroom tiles, and in the sound of students running down the hallway. I cried in this bathroom because

Reunion

Brad drew a picture of me that was 99 percent nose and told me I was ugly. I kissed my first boyfriend outside of the gym locker room because he passed me a note that read: *Kiss after gym?* I felt intense jealousy when my friends made new friends, and abject hopelessness when my boyfriend and I broke up, which we did often and unkindly. I was loud and opinionated, often rude and overbearing, and undiagnosed with inattentive ADHD and anxiety that made my brain a series of fun house mirrors. Stepping into the school for parent-teacher conferences as the parent meant revisiting the same places where hormones ran high and interpersonal effectiveness was low, classrooms and lockers where the hidden versions of myself and thousands of strangers are stored like invisible avatars, where the scent in the air is the unmistakable aroma of over one hundred years of adolescent tumult, and no amount of ammonia can get rid of it. We are not who we were in high school, and yet, that version of oneself remains somewhere inside each of us like a nesting doll.

This is the perfect topic for therapy, but, as usual, I spent the first forty-eight minutes telling Allen that everything was fine, and the final two minutes of our time together emotionally exploding. Erin had received an email about the twenty-year reunion and forwarded it to me and Gene and Cara with the sentence "See you there???" though more a directive than a question.

"Time is just . . . it's going so fast," I choked out. Allen smiled at me warmly, nodding in agreement.

"It tends to do that in middle age."

•   •   •

BAD VIBES ONLY

I am not one to object to being called middle-aged. Given that my father died at age sixty-four, I could be well past the halfway point of my own life. And given that I watched my first husband die when he was just thirty-five years old, any year to come is a gift. But there it is: we are middle-aged. *I am middle-aged.* The options for who I will be are getting slimmer with every passing year, and my shame in who I have been is only slightly dissipating with years of therapy and journaling and doing embarrassing things like talking to my former selves and saying, "I forgive you. You're okay."

"See you there!" I reply to Erin, and I save the date. The next few months are a flurry of text messages among the four of us:

> *Do you think that {redacted} will be there?*
> > *Didn't {redacted} go to prison?*
> *That was a rumor.*
> > *GUYS!!!! What if {redacted} is there! I had the biggest crush on him!*

In preparation, we spent months reviewing our yearbooks and opening the musty shoeboxes of photos and notes we'd been storing under our beds and in the backs of our closets for two decades, texting one another our findings. Our graduating class was just 120 people, and three of us have died. Justin had pancreatic cancer, Eddie had a brain tumor, and Erin had complications from cystic fibrosis. We did not know this on our last day of high school, when we emptied the contents of our lockers into trash bags and sat on the steps signing yearbooks. We did not know that, as we were wishing one another luck, we would need it. My own mind flips between an incredible tenderness for all these children and the adults they were lucky to have become . . . and remembering when I see a yearbook inscription that reads, poetically, "Suck my dick" that yeah, Tyler *was* an asshole. Maybe he still is, actually, even though a brief internet search tells me that he is a married father of three. Husbands and dads can also be jerks!

As the months pass, my friends and I build up an extremely casual event into an emotional powder keg, and we egg on one another's anxieties. We repeatedly quiz Cara on the order of her boyfriends and whether there was any overlap (there was). We remind Gene of the time he threw up Wheaties in the hallway outside the science building and the janitor made him clean it up himself. We use every memory to fuel our predictions for this reunion: we imagine emotional reunions with long-lost friends, possible affairs with unrequited crushes, and potential altercations with nearly forgotten rivals.

What we don't imagine is the three-day reunion weekend kicking off with a golf tournament where the average player is aged sixty-five. Gene and Erin and I made a golf foursome with our friend Margaret, who was the taller, smarter, and more athletically gifted version of me in high school. Margaret had been one of the founding members of our girls' golf team, established in 1998 when the boys' coach decided that one year of trying to coach teenage girls who wanted to spend their time on the course asking him how he met his wife and what her name was and what he was going to get her for their anniversary "wasn't working for him." We were, at one point, the worst team in the state of Minnesota. This was in part because we competed in a league filled with girls from real, WASP-y prep schools. Our competitors spent their weekends playing at country clubs with their parents and practiced after school at clubs where the yearly membership fees were exponentially higher than our school tuition. Our team teed off before the school day on a public course that was bisected by active train tracks. We were regularly penalized for swearing (me and Erin) or throwing clubs (also me) and were also . . . just bad at the sport. But today, twenty years after our final high school match, we are basically professional golfers. We can't believe our skills, and we can't believe it when a cart pulls up next to us with four of our classmates: former sports stars who now have receding hairlines contrasting their still-boyish faces. We hug, we pose for photos, and we suck in our stomachs. *Huh*, I think, *look at us! Everything is fine!*

It's tacky to show up drunk to a reunion, or to drink too much *at* a reunion. I don't like the way alcohol affects me: even one drink makes my stomach hurt, but I spent plenty of years powering through the pain and blacking it out entirely. Drunk people tend to annoy me, but when *you're* blackout drunk, nothing annoys you! Either way, I know I won't be drinking at the reunion. I say as much when I get to Cara's house to do what we always did together before school events: "Get ready." Erin had spread yearbooks and faded notes across Cara's kitchen island, and Cara created a playlist of our favorite songs from our high school years: Next, K-Ci & JoJo, Destiny's Child, 112, NSYNC. I turn down the offer of a beer, wine, or hard seltzer, and crack an ice-cold sparkling water filled with delicious artificial flavors. My nerves have started:

Reunion

What if the net result of this evening is that all my former classmates confess to hating me, to have *always* hated me? What if I'm neither Romy nor Michele but instead the terrible girl who tormented both of them in high school, whose adult life turns out to be a sham? I don't *think* this is true, but then again, every time I take the Harry Potter house quiz, it's clear that I'm a Slytherin.

I was already dressed and made up, but apparently the natural makeup look I'd opted for was just a bit too natural. "Come on up," Cara says, ushering me to her bedroom, "we have *lots* of makeup."

And this was where I made the mistake of saying to myself, *Surely you can take an edible before you leave.*

Marijuana was absolutely out of the question for me in high school. I had committed to saying no to drugs in Drug Abuse Resistance Education in fifth grade, when a Minneapolis cop came into our classroom and passed around what he claimed were real drugs confiscated from real criminals. We handled the baggies as if they were live grenades whose explosion could instantly drop us into a life of disrepute. Marijuana, Officer Olson told us, would make you lazy and fat. Cocaine, however, would make you feel like God. Both were bad, though, and his lessons stuck with me at least until college, when I decided that a person who has done keg stands in an asbestos-filled basement wasn't exactly "too classy" to take the occasional unidentified substance from a stranger (if my children are reading this, never do this, your mother was an idiot). Now, as an adult woman in a state where it's been legalized, the medicinal power of THC has quelled my anxiety, helped me sleep at night, and been a nice little treat.

With just a little nibble of what looks a lot like a gummy vitamin, I feel enveloped in a safe little cloud of happiness, fully conversational and at ease. It's like putting on a pair of rose-colored glasses that make everyone and everything around me both interesting and lovable. Wouldn't that be the best version of me to present tonight? The version who is not nervous or awkward but warm and inviting? Yes, I agree with myself, and scrounge through my purse until I find what I'm looking for.

The reunion is in the gym, which looks exactly as you might imagine it. The harsh overhead lights are in full force, rendering our makeup useless. The sound of hundreds of people shouting over one another bounces around the cavernous space, and we scan the multigenerational crowds celebrating their thirtieth or fortieth or fiftieth or sixtieth reunions for anyone remotely close to our age. This evening is shaping up to be a bust: there is hardly anyone from our year here tonight, the appetizers are bags of chips placed on the folding tables, and the bonfire we were promised is canceled due to both the fire hazard and the rainstorm that started as we walked in. And that's when it hits me, hard: I am not safe in a warm cloud of comfort, I am irreparably and undeniably high.

It turns out that the edible I took was not the single dose that makes me feel heavenly, but a double dose that has separated my brain from my body entirely. While my body is . . . somewhere . . . my brain is up in the rafters looking down at me. *Nora*, she whispers, *you're smiling too much*. *No*, she corrects, *you're not smiling enough*. I'm also speaking slowly or possibly too loudly? I'm very, very thirsty, but convincing my feet and legs to move the rest of my body forward feels nonnegotiable. I mistakenly make eye contact with a group of men from the class of '55, some of whom I recognize from the golf course. They are so little, like a group of lawn gnomes, their faces somehow smoothed to look like shiny white and pink pebbles.

"Women are so tall now!" one of them shouts up to me, and I nod.

"It's terrible!" I agree, and they laugh.

But really it is terrible: my legs are too long, and my head is up way too high. I want to find a small amount of solid ground, where I can curl up and wait for this to pass. I excuse myself from my petite suitors and try to find an escape route through the crowd and toward the only safe place in any high school: the girls' bathroom. Unfortunately, my gym teacher is there, and she cannot, must not, know that I am high. She could tell my mom—they go to church together sometimes!—I could be expelled posthumously. Wait, that means you're dead. I'm not dead. But I might be. I might be a ghost haunting this school. Instead of walking around Ms. Barry—I will never call her by her first name—I've walked directly into her, and while she is having a very impassioned conversation with me, I am wishing I knew what we were talking about. I can tell from reading her face when I should nod in agreement or laugh, but I cannot for the life of me get my brain to tell my mouth to say anything until I finally blurt out, "I need to sit down!" and feel my arms jerk forward to pull out a seat at a round table set for ten and occupied by nine members of the class of '81. To avoid them speaking to or noticing me, I pick up my phone and text Matthew.

Please get me not high.

    Excuse me?

I took an edible and it was too much.

    God dammit. Sorry honey, you just have to wait it out.

I cannot do that. Please advise.

He stops returning my texts, but I do not stop sending them. He needs to be kept apprised of the situation, and the only part of this night that makes sense are my thumbs, who have not betrayed me and deftly dart across the keyboard with a play-by-play of the evening as it unfolds around me. A small group from our graduating class has found one another and gathered around me, where I remain seated.

"Sorry," I say, "I can't get up." They pretend that makes sense and gather around me for a group photo. I can sense—or am imagining it in my THC-soaked brain—a nervous energy crackling among us like electricity before a lightning strike. I see in all these middle-aged faces a certainty that each of us is Romy or Michele, a high school outcast trying to be perceived the way we'd like to be. But there is no need for that, truly. The passage of two decades has made us older and softer, has dulled all our sharp edges. There will be no confrontations, no revenge of the nerds, no drunken ex-boyfriends proclaiming their love. There is no reason for any of us to pretend that we invented Post-its or that life is better than it is: as a development worker drunkenly reveals to us, he already knows how much we pay in property taxes and how much we're worth, and it ain't much.

The only drama of this evening is taking place in my own brain as I try to convince my body to metabolize the THC faster. I'm so desperately curious about my former classmates: not just where they are now but where they've been for the past twenty years. How have their hearts been broken? What dreams have been dashed or accomplished? I want so badly to know that the decades between who we were and who we are have been kind to them, that they have gotten what they need and hopefully what they want. It takes hours for me to feel normal-ish, and by that time we've moved to a nearby restaurant, where I'm sitting next to a boy whose eyebrows were ahead of his time in 2001. Unlike me, he has maintained his composure all evening, and has provided me with a decent summary of the classmates in attendance. "Isn't it awesome," he says with a sincerity that makes me want to cry, "to see how everyone turned out?"

Drinking to excess has always given me the dubious gift of deleting large portions of the evening. But THC does the opposite: it crystallizes every moment into a clear picture in my brain. So when I wake up the next morning, snuggled up next to Erin in Cara's spare bedroom, I groan into my pillow, remembering how I hobbled to the bathroom stall and stared at my feet for a half hour. How I stood mute in the middle of a conversation between two people discussing the parish priests of the southern Minneapolis suburbs, replying, "Oh, nobody cares" when, during a pause in the conversation, one woman asked how I've been. How, when seeing our friend Ariana, I told her, "You always thought you were an awkward side character, but no. You were our Jennifer Aniston." How I insisted that my friend Justin's wife was too pretty to be real, which might sound rude but is 100 percent true, and in the future, I will run for president on a platform that caps and redistributes human beauty. How we sat in our old chemistry classroom, staring out the window at downtown Minneapolis, the Mississippi River flowing by. "It was Eden," a classmate said wistfully. "The kind of beauty you can't see when you're in it." How, sitting in that bathroom stall, I rested my head against the baby-blue wall and texted my friends an apology I could have sent twenty years before:

I'm sorry. I really didn't want to be like this.

10

Stay-At-Home Mom

I've pretended a lot of things to get a man to like me; I've constructed entirely new personalities to reflect the interests and desires of a man I barely even desired. I'd deny this, should you ask me in public, but there was a brief, dark few months my senior year in college where I was a conservative Republican in hopes of getting a boy who played club lacrosse to call me his girlfriend instead of just calling me at one a.m. to see if I wanted to make out (I did!).

You might think that being married means no longer pretending to like the things you do not, but in the case of my marriage, you would be incorrect. Marriage is about compromise: sometimes you're the person working to debunk your partner's preferences and sometimes you're the person swallowing your distaste and pretending. I know what kind of music Matthew likes to listen to: it's loud and angry and sounds like sad boys yelling at their disinterested fathers. But I still put on Top 40 hits whenever I get the chance, and after enough plays, he'll drum along and find something to like about it. I accept and love Matthew in spite of his distaste for soft cheeses and the fact that he refuses any and all salad dressings, instead eating a bowl of vegetables without so much as a drizzle of olive oil. Matthew knows I am not a person who wants to leave the house, but he still puts forth his best effort to try to convince me that there is a whole wide world outside our front door. It's one thing to pretend to be fiscally *and* morally conservative; it's another to pretend to like traveling, because the latter may require you *go* somewhere, and I am simply not a person who likes to go places or do things. I'm a person who is happiest in one place, and that place is my house. I might sometimes sit on the couch a bit differently to switch things up, but my ideal travel experience is the thirty seconds it takes to get from my bedroom to the living room with a quick pit stop in the kitchen for coffee and a spoonful of Nutella for breakfast.

I'm not *afraid* to travel. I'm not an individual who prays when a plane takes off and applauds when it lands, although I love the idea of cheering at the end of air travel because how have we become so jaded that we aren't absolutely dazzled by our ability to propel a heavy metal tube through the atmosphere, transporting us across land and sea while we watch TV and eat snacks? I've had the same number of travel mishaps as any other person: luggage lost, flights canceled, comically small rental cars that feel as though they could be swept from the highway by a gust of wind. But typically the things that go wrong when I travel are my own fault.

When Ralph was just three years old, I booked a trip to New York City for our blended family so everyone could watch Matthew and I run the New York City half-marathon on behalf of the American Cancer Society. Running is an exaggeration; picture a shuffle step for 13.1 miserable miles. We got to the ticket counter to check in and were informed that I'd booked *my* flight for the present day, while my child and soon-to-be husband would be flying the next day. How this was possible we still do not know. I swore up and down that I'd booked our flights for the same day, but a computer reservation system has no reason to lie, and in the end, I walked through the TSA line trying to ignore the cries from my abandoned toddler. Another year, I stepped up to the rental car counter in a new city with all four of our kids in tow and realized that I hadn't *actually* booked a rental car. When my sister turned thirty-nine and decided *this* was the year she wanted to splash out and celebrate, I arrived for my flight to Las Vegas only to find—you guessed it—I hadn't booked a ticket at all. But these mishaps aren't even why I don't love to travel; it's that travel is just so much *doing*, and I don't want to *do* anything.

It's a family trait; if my children or I are already seated, we'll cry out for anyone who is standing to bring us a glass of water or a phone charger. Our youngest child will cry out from the toilet, "Can anyone wipe my butt?" *Anyone.* Doesn't matter who! He'll take a butt wipe from any living person, so long as he doesn't have to do it himself. More than once I've called a child into my room, where I'm already tucked under the covers for a day of work, to ask them if they can grab the book that's on the dresser on the other side of the room, or retrieve a pen that's rolled under the bed. It's understood within our family that if you dare to stand up during a family movie night, you are now the messenger who will bring back hydration, sustenance, and lip balm for the entire family.

And yet, Matthew's hope for a change of my homebody heart persists. "You know," he'll say, "when I traveled for work, I had a fun rule." I'm skeptical at the idea of a "fun rule" but he continues, using the higher-pitched voice he uses with our children when trying to convince them to take more than just a weekly shower. "My fun rule was that I wouldn't stay at a chain hotel unless it was the only option . . . and I'd never eat a dinner at the hotel. That way, I could always make sure I saw something new, even if I was in a city that didn't *seem* exciting!"

"Wow!" I say. "That sounds really fun for you!" But not for me! Because if I travel for work, I stay in the same chain of hotels and order the same dinner to my room, where I hopefully have two queen beds: one for eating and working, one for sleeping. I'll spend the next few hours watching reality TV shows I've already seen, and then fall asleep, wake up, and go to the airport to eat the same travel breakfast I eat every single time. If I've traveled correctly, the interruption to my life has been minimal, and I can slip back into my regular life as if nothing has happened.

Still, every time I check in while I'm on a work trip, Matthew will "check in" and ask me the same questions:

What's your plan for the day?

Where are you getting dinner?

Have you heard of {attraction I most certainly have not heard of}?

He never (outwardly) judges me when I tell him my plan is not going to change and I am going to eat a hotel cheeseburger in my pajamas, so please don't contact me again until I'm home. Matthew (lovingly??) calls my condition "*anora*phobia," and he is working tirelessly to find new treatment options. He believes the cure for my affliction could be exposure, which is why he does things like book a day trip to Tucson, about an hour's drive from where we live in Phoenix. I was under the impression that the hour-long drive to a new city was the "trip" and that the rest of our time away would be spent in the hotel room watching Bravo and ordering in tacos. Matthew had other, more interactive plans: he'd selected a few brunch spots and hikes, and had mapped out some shops he thought I would like. I stared longingly at the bed.

"It's ten thirty a.m., you really want to sit in this room for twenty-four hours until checkout?"

"Ideally, twenty-four and a half hours. Checkout is eleven, right?"

We went to brunch, and it was lovely and I ate quickly so I could get back to the hotel, take off my pants, and lie back down. But I could tell that in this case, our marriage was more important than my habits, and so we walked around the city for hours, dipping into bookstores and record shops and gift shops so we could placate our children with gifts upon our return. *Then* we got down to business and watched old episodes of *Real Housewives of New York*. By the time we left—exactly 24.5 hours after we arrived—I *loved* Tucson. I could see myself living there! I can see myself living nearly anywhere I've been: the coast of Ireland, the farmland in eastern Colorado, the suburbs of Detroit. This happens everywhere I've been. In every place I've visited, I could easily see myself sitting inside on a sofa in another city, scrolling the internet and writing and looking up the criminal records of people from my past whose names I've just remembered. Once I'm back home, I love where I was. But it's just that the getting there takes so long, and by the time I've gotten on and off a plane or in and out of a car, I feel like I've done enough. If I *have* to leave my house, the best kind of travel means limiting any and all motion to the travel itself. After five days in a cabin up north, Matthew asked me if I was interested in any day trips with the kids. He'd scouted out possible hikes and historic landmarks. I'd already scouted out the couch situation and opened a stack of books. I would not be leaving the cabin—our *trip*—for a side adventure whose outcome was entirely unknown! When we took our oldest kids and Matthew's parents to Ireland, I was more than content to spend my days sitting on a couch in our rental cottage reading. I was *being* in Ireland, but Matthew and the rest of the family needed to pile into the rental van and *see* Ireland.

Like my nose, I get this from my father, another creature of habit who was matched with a traveler and a doer. Since our father died, our mother has maxed out travel visas in Italy and Ireland, tooling around the countries on her own, visiting old friends and making new ones. My father—lucky him—would rather be dead. As kids, any trips we took were limited to driving distances, meaning anything within twenty-four hours of drive time. Our mom would find a decrepit "resort"—often a collection of rotting single-wide trailers on the shores of a lake somewhere—and pack us up in the car. Our dad would stay behind, no matter how hard we begged him to join us.

"No thanks," he'd say. "I had enough travel when I went to Vietnam." It took us a few years to realize that his "trip" to Vietnam was for a war, and more years to realize that going to war in a foreign country when you're seventeen years old is likely to fuck you up. After two tours in Vietnam, Dad was done traveling for the most part. He liked to be comfortable, he liked to be home. My mother would book international trips with her high school girlfriends, and my father would book himself a tee time at the municipal golf course where he was a regular. Had my mother died first, our father would have spent his days the same way he'd spent them for the entirety of their marriage: waking up, reading the paper, heading to the golf course, returning for lunch, sitting in his office for hours, and emerging for dinner and more reading before watching crappy reality TV and going to bed before ten p.m., breaking occasionally to call and complain about the lack of dinners being prepared for him. Instead, he is at eternal rest in the city of his birthplace, just a few miles from the house where he was born, the house where he died, and the golf course where he spent the sixty-four years in between.

For just shy of forty years, my mother did what she liked to do (travel, go to parties, socialize with friends and strangers) and my dad did what he liked to do (golf, read, watch TV, judge people from a distance), and the overlap in the Venn diagram of their marriage was living in the same house and raising their children together. Forty years of marriage feels statistically improbable for me and Matthew, but we can aim for the same kind of harmony my parents had, an understanding that the ties that bind us are something bigger than shared interests or hobbies or even taste in music, food, or movies. I had insisted we write our wedding vows ourselves, yet I have no memory or record of what we promised each other that day. But does it matter? Because the promise of marriage is that we will stay beside each other, grow together, hold each other up when things are hard. And I swear I will, as long as I can also stay home.

11

Is This Good?

Our eight-year-old has spent five whole days without me on a road trip to San Diego with his cousins and aunts and uncles and grandma. This is a big step for him, a boy who prefers to be within arm's reach of his mother at all times, who looks into my eyes and says, "I will never leave you" with a seriousness that both rewards and unnerves me. He has called me every night from his grandmother's phone to say good night and remind me that he loves me and misses me and will be home in just a few sleeps. But today, on his return trip home, he is calling because he is in the middle of a deep moral dilemma: his uncle is stopping for lunch at a restaurant that conflicts with my child's principles.

"Tell him it's okay if he eats here once," Grandma says, but instead I tell him that it's perfectly fine if he doesn't want to eat food from a restaurant that invalidates the rights of the people he loves, and that he can kindly request that his uncle go through another drive-through and delay their return trip a whopping five minutes. He returns home a few hours later absolutely starving, but beaming with pride.

"I didn't eat it, Mom! I wouldn't do it!"

This is my child's first foray into social activism, and he is already hooked on the superiority of it all. I'm glad he's not on Twitter, because he would be drunk on the binary thinking. Instead, he is now in the back seat of my car, peppering me with the same question over and over, applied to everything he consumes: Is this good?

Is this good? he asks, pointing at his favorite big-box re-tailer. Yes, I start to say, they provide a decent starting wage, make an effort to stock smaller brands, and donate lots of money to local organizations. But . . . they are also famously anti-union and have appeared to rip off small designers and makers more than once.

Is this good? He is pointing at his shoes, which were made in Cambodia and likely by a child his age. But . . . are also very affordable?

Is this good? He is asking about Christianity itself! As a whole! Which has given many people (including myself) a connection to God and also . . . well . . . genocide, patriarchy, the Crusades, residential schools . . .

I successfully change the topic by putting on a podcast, but long after we've left the car, that question rings in my mind. *Is this good?* Stepping foot onto the internet will con-vince anyone that the only way to think is in black and white: people and brands and movements are all good or bad, us or them. And the *us* fractures so quickly along so many lines that it is hard to believe that anything could be good at all. I once posted a photo of my daughter's ninth-grade math homework and called it a "cursed image," a playful joke based on my own deep-seated anxiety over having a brain that doesn't seem to see or understand basic numbers. I regularly wake from nightmares where I've stepped back into my high school math classroom to take a test I'm not prepared for, the numbers swimming on the page before me. I got a message in response to this photo:

> *I'm disappointed to see someone in your position take such a narrow-minded view and perpetuate math shaming. It's hard enough being a teacher in this climate.*

I hadn't said that math was bad, or attempted to shame math for not making sense to me, but it didn't matter. I was already an enemy in the War for Math, the context of my own personal experience irrelevant when compared to the imagined impact this could have had on a person who was *this close* to becoming a Math Enthusiast and was deterred from pursuing a career in STEM by my careless caption. This is a small and inconsequential example, but do you need more if you've been alive for the past two or three presidential elections? Don't you know it when you see it, this fervent need we have to sort one another and everything around us into good and bad? Can't you feel it, when you see someone or something is wrong, and you reach out to correct it? A woman I know casually once chided a person for parking in a disabled parking space without the proper documentation. The offending parker was later revealed to have multiple sclerosis; she'd forgotten her hangtag but still wanted to go to Target.

The online therapy app that makes therapy affordable and accessible to populations who might not otherwise have access to mental healthcare also underpays its therapists and might just be selling user data to advertisers. My hybrid saves hundreds of gallons of fossil fuels every year while also reassuring me that I'm a Good Person. However, the batteries are toxic to dispose of and are created with rare earth metals that are obtained either through dangerous mining practices, warfare, or maybe just scraping the bottom of our ocean? My Shih Tzu is on antidepressants that have helped her come out from under the bed and actually interact with us . . . and some actual human people can't afford access to mental healthcare. Fast fashion is one of our biggest environmental hazards . . . and it also makes stylish, trendy clothing accessible to people with limited budgets who can't afford to shop ethically sourced, handmade, small-batch clothing. A person I know in real life who has shown me and my family kindness made a boneheaded professional move that was revealed publicly. His decision had been self-preserving and ungenerous, but hardly cruel or illegal. The Twitter replies referred to him as "garbage," "a piece of shit," and "worthless."

Never in human history has it been so easy to spy on one another, to look through the windows we've all left wide open in our own lives and take inventory of each other's thoughts, feelings, and values, and to analyze and assign worth and intent, to respond quickly and decisively to the actions of other people, to treat them like they are faceless entities when we can see their (filtered) faces right on our screen. We do this—I do this—and justify it by saying it's to be expected. That if someone shares something—anything—publicly, they're inviting discourse about their intentions and their impact. If they didn't want the attention, why did they court it?

I would like to propose a radical old idea that many people have been practicing for thousands of years: nearly everything on this earth and in it is good and bad. Republicans? Democrats? Capitalism? Kohl's Doorbuster sales? Christianity? Nearly everything you can think of is helpful to some and harmful to others. Therapists call this both/and thinking, and there's a reason why it isn't as popular as tribalism and judgment: it's time-consuming, tedious, and unsatisfying. It does nothing to elevate our blood pressure and, more important, it does not reward our need to be right. Personally, I love to be right! I love to boil a complex issue down to its simplest parts and cleave it apart for proper sorting: villains to the right, heroes to the left. In a world filled with overwhelming issues, our tendency toward a binary does not surprise me. What could be more soothing than knowing things are either one thing or the other? Who can stand to tax their aching brains with more critical thought, with exploring the nuances of a topic when we can simply make a snap decision and be done with it already? I hate to describe critical thinking as a privilege, but take a look around: life is hard, and people are tired, and the small doses of camaraderie and dopamine we get from clicking "reshare" on a hot take will always be easier and more satisfying than reading a well-researched piece of reporting and thinking aloud to yourself, "Well, it certainly seems like a complex issue."

I do not have my child's moral resolve. I know that Jeff Bezos and Amazon are, to put it gently—not good—and yet I click that Buy Now button as though I'm a person who doesn't live within ten minutes of any kind of store a person could imagine. They're also the largest book retailer, and I shouldn't slander them in a book when I'll also rely on them to get this product into your hands. I know that factory farming is *bad* and fast food is *addictive*, but when I'm very tired and the idea of dinner feels like too much to handle, I am inclined to pull into our favorite fast-food restaurant and order our usual. I keep the bags shut tight to keep in the heat and the smell, and I imagine how excited the kids will be to see their drive-through dinner.

Is this good? Depending on who you ask, this is a company with a generous starting salary and college tuition benefits or an evil multinational corporation rife with labor violations. Probably both, and the fries are excellent.

12

Competitive Parenting Association

We're thrilled to welcome you to the Competitive Parenting Association, the only organization dedicated to the sport of raising children and reinforcing the parental ego.

Sports typically require that rules and objectives are agreed upon beforehand. In football, for example, the objective is to score a touchdown, and in the middle there is lots of pushing and what looks like physical assault. In baseball, you want to make it around all the bases, and there is a lot of standing around. Soccer is a lot of running and some falling, and also, if we're lucky, a few points here and there. In the end, there's usually a winner and a loser and the scoreboard tells the final story. The benefits of team sports are well-documented: they build character and community and resilience, give you endorphins, and promote heart health! But there's a new sport that has gained popularity over the past three decades, mostly among women. It offers absolutely no health benefits, the rules are confusing and ever-changing, and the objective is very unclear. Like golf, tennis, and polo, it takes time and money and is inclusive in theory only because privilege is the primary form of mass transit for white people, a metaphorical bus that takes you a few stops farther than your own parents, burning the fossil fuel of nepotism.

What used to be a sacred responsibility that reflected the growing relationship between you and your child is now an opportunity to show up and show off while comparing yourself to friends and strangers. It's absolutely miserable, and while there are plenty of other parents in the world (and maybe even in your life), you need to know that this is an individual sport. Just a few generations ago, you may have lived with extended family, sharing the responsibility of caring for and nursing a small person. But now it's all on you, honey!

Here's an important note to remember: your partner has also joined the CPA, **but you are in no way teammates and your points will be accrued on an individual basis**. However—and people really don't like this rule—your partner's mistakes can and will detract from your overall score. A distinct advantage is given to men, because our cultural bar for parenthood is so low that simply being around your child for any extended amount of time is enough to consider you a "good father." Should you change a diaper or groom your child in any way, confetti will rain from the heavens and a statue shall be erected in your honor. Is this sexist and outdated? Deeply!

If you're wondering, what about single parents? Well, what about them? The same arbitrary rules apply to any person in charge of the care and development of a young person, and you will be doubly penalized for any shortcomings real or imagined with absolutely no lenience for what we will refer to ambiguously and insultingly as "your situation."

Competitive Parenting Association

We hope that the following pages provide you with the guidance you need to be successful in this new endeavor, as we all know that success is the only measure of value for ourselves and our offspring.

WHERE DO I START?

The first thing you need to do once your baby is on the way is let people *know*. We recommend hiring a videographer to hide in the bushes while you lead your partner out onto the front lawn so they can see the skywriting drone you've hired to write PREGNANT across your sliver of sky. The videographer can have the clips scored and sized for Instagram in forty-eight hours so you can announce this to friends from grade school whom you'd deliberately avoid in the grocery store, former clients, colleagues, and people you met at a party in 2014. Your uncle doesn't use Instagram, so hopefully someone calls him.

In preparation for becoming a parent, you probably read a book. You didn't need to. You only needed to *buy* the books and place them on your nightstand, where they make a great photo for Instagram and a daily reminder that you are a good person. But don't forget that there are plenty of new purchases coming up. You'll need a new car, because how can a baby fit into a sedan designed to hold five adults?? It can't, so you'll need a massive SUV. You'll probably want to move because babies absolutely prefer to be surrounded by several thousand square feet while they're spending twenty hours a day sleeping. But before you make any of these choices, you need to get yourself online and scroll through the lives of people who make their money by looking good on the internet. Here you'll see that some of the many things you'll need in order to prove

"I Love My Kid This Many Dollars' Worth" (a supplemental e-course available on our website) include a robotic baby swing that costs more than a car payment, a selection of organic onesies in various shades of "baby diarrhea," and a three-hundred-dollar wicker basket just like the one Moses was found in (was Moses the first influencer? Food for thought!).

Points

Obviously, you want more points than any other parent, and to accrue them at any cost. Documentation is the easiest way to get on the scoreboard, and at this point it should come naturally to you. You're already accustomed to posting your own comings and goings online, but now you have a helpless and non-consenting new person to post about! The world needs to know when they arrived (date and time), their full name (no middle initials!), and how (vaginal birth? C-section? Surrogacy?). Make sure to describe exactly how much pain Mom was in and to describe her as a "rock star." Every like, share, and comment is not only a point but a sign that you're a good parent. The growth and development of a child offers boundless opportunities for content. Every milestone is an opportunity to show off your child's new tooth or new trick. But simply documenting isn't going to get you to the top of the leaderboard, you'll need to share your child's achievements so everyone knows how superior you are to other families. Baby walks early? Points! You sign baby up for music? Points! Baby wears only earth-tone neutrals made from reclaimed deadstock organic cotton starting at forty-eight dollars for a pair of leggings? Points! Points! Points! Remember, quitters never win, and parents can't let their kids quit!

BUT WHAT KIND OF A PARENT DO I WANT TO BE?

At the CPA, we know this question is a big one. And that's why we recommend committing to a specific league within our association and committing as soon as possible. Leagues follow their own unique rules and point systems, based around a common ideology decided upon by the parents and subject to immense change without notice. Don't wait for your child to show their own unique needs, decide right away what kind of parent you are, and shout it from the rooftops of the internet!

Here is a sampling of some of our more popular leagues. Please note that the vast majority of people do *not* join the same league as their co-parent, as being on the same page about raising your children is both boring and unrealistic.

Q-Amoms: *Are* vaccines necessary, or could polio build character in our kids? These parents are just *asking questions* and *pushing back* against the *establishment*. They're big into dried beans, carob chips, certain kinds of Christianity, homeschooling, organic food, and natural birth. The content here is all about how your choices are just *best for your kid.* He naturally loves vegetables and asks for kale chips as a snack. She has a favorite brand of hummus. They don't wear shoes because shoes are just foot coffins, and our ancestors knew the value of a rusty nail in the bottom of a toe. If your kids are free-range but also not allowed to watch Disney movies because the plotlines are filled with gayness and communism, this is the league where you'll thrive!

Alpha Dads: Parenting is women's work, and any participation outside of physical and emotional abuse will lose you points. Don't be a pussy about it, you little bitch.

Sports: A sports-based league within the sport of parenting? Now you've heard it all! If you love excellence, this might be the track for you. Regardless of your child's talent, you'll spend hours of every weeknight sitting on the sidelines during their practices and games to prove that you love them. As they grow, your calendar will revolve around weekend tournaments and your once fashionable wardrobe will be replaced with a vast collection that comprises every promotional item for the many expensive teams your children are forced to participate in. You'll invest more than a year's worth of college tuition into camp and league fees hoping that it will turn into a college scholarship. Statistically speaking, it will not, and all the time and money you've invested in forcing your child to turn a passing interest into your passion would have been better spent on a 529 account. Whether or not your child shows any physical promise, you should secure a coach or a trainer before they lose their first tooth. Refer to this as "opening doors" or "finding opportunities." Allow yourself the thrill of living through your child, knowing that five is not too young to find a passion and commit to it and that their trophies are your trophies too, so find a place in your house where *everyone* can see them!

Half-Ass: Not everyone can give 110 percent to their kids. We get it, and yes we look down on you for it.

But this specific league caters to those who need a low bar (and still might not clear it). Consider this league if you pride yourself on running late and forgetting Spirit Day, if you can see yourself dropping your kid off at school during a teacher in-service day because you just don't read the school emails, or if your child knows most of the swear words before they can recite the alphabet. Your child *can* recite the alphabet, can't they?

Spon-Moms: It used to be that only celebrity kids could make an income. By the grace of God, now any child can become a profit center. The world of spon offers so many avenues for building wealth around your child: create a YouTube channel where you document their journey through puberty, or film them opening toys. Incorporate their intimate childhood moments into sponsored stories and swipe-ups, custom discount codes and affiliate links. A small up-front investment in birthing or adopting a child can reap huge dividends for parents with the dedication to documentation. Let your imagination run wild (and your kids, as long as they're camera ready and the product is clearly visible!).

Best Friends: Boundaries are boring, and "Mom and Dad" are what your parents are called, not you! You're more than *just* a mom: you're a confidante, a pal, and a secretly jealous competitor. Your friends can't believe that you and your daughter are still wearing matching outfits, and your daughter can't believe it either because she asked you like ten times to stop buying the same clothes as her. Your son might have a girlfriend, but at least she looks just like you, and besides, you could break them up if you really wanted to.

Morally Superior: Nobody likes you, but you don't care. Why would you want to fit into a culture where babies are picked up by their parents without their consent, where they're fed conventionally grown vegetables and factory-farmed meat *which, by the way, is murder*. Your kids wear your views on their onesies, so everyone at the playground knows that breast is best and that a woman's place is in the house *and* the senate.

Drunk Moms: Dads who drink this much would be called alcoholics, but when it's wine o'clock, Mommy needs her mommy juice, and when they whine, you wine . . . get it? It's all in good fun, because alcohol is legal and you don't *drive* anywhere while you're drinking unless it's a mommy meetup with an open bar, in which case you have like three drinks max, and besides, you bought them the expensive car seats! Toddlers *are* monsters, but when they have the fine motor skills to get you a glass of water while you're puking in the toilet, it all pays off.

HOW LONG IS MY MEMBERSHIP VALID?

For life, baby!

Speaking of babies, this phase is where you'll feel like LeBron playing pickup at the YMCA. It's not hard to dunk on people when you've got the time and resources the global majority could only dream of, and you'll find your child comfortably in the top percentile of anything measurable by a pediatrician.

By the time your kid is ready for school and has smashed those major milestones, you might feel like your score has slowed down. Don't worry! You can rack up serious points by enrolling them in a school with "unique programming," like a charter or magnet school that has a time-consuming application process. Montessori is fine, but Waldorf or Country Day are more expensive and every tuition dollar equals a point, and besides, aren't kids worth it? Not financially, of course. Most childless adults will end up saving *way* more money, but eventually you *can* monetize your child and earn points and dollars (one more reason to join the Spon-Mom league!).

We know the teenage years are hard and that many modern children are showing signs of "mental illness" or "neurodivergence" and—*ick, ew*—that sounds hard. But remember that perception is everything, and mind over matter, and maybe their minds don't matter at all! Or certainly not as much as their appearance. Your children's wins are your wins, their failures are aberrations that can be rectified with a call to the manager or the right check written to the right organization. And as your child grows, so too does the potential of their—your!—wins. Remember to push them toward interests that are the right balance of esoteric and easily mastered, to fill out applications for colleges whose names absolutely reek with success, and toward careers that are highly lucrative even if they are morally bankrupt. Once your children become parents, you can also accumulate points through *their* children. After all, those children wouldn't exist without you, it's only fair!

WHAT IF I DON'T WANT TO PARTICIPATE?

We don't care! Try as you might to keep your eyes on your own paper and your focus on your own child, you will be surrounded by competitive parents who will use your children as yardsticks to indicate their own children's success or failure. There's no such thing as a tie or a draw, and even nonparticipation is a form of participation.

Please do not reach out with comments, questions, or concerns. The game is on.

13

Unravel with Me

My favorite category of YouTube video is a Get Ready With Me, where a young person will train a camera on their face during their morning routine, narrating their actions and releasing their inner monologue for the benefit of their invisible audience. At the end, you've watched a sleepy twentysomething transform into a sexy twentysomething, and you have some aspirational new products to try. It's the exact opposite of how I start my own days, which I would categorize as an instantaneous coming apart as I gain consciousness.

Anxiety is a serious and sometimes debilitating mental health issue that affects millions of people worldwide, but when you're, say, trying to explain to another person who has not fallen down the spiral staircase of your worst thoughts why exactly you're unable to walk through a grocery store without imagining every single can, shelf, and cart rotting in a future landfill, poisoning our soil and returning as radioactive carrots and kale, you have to admit that it's also . . . a little embarrassing. I'm embarrassed for myself every time anxiety loosens its grip on my brain, even when I'm the only witness to the thoughts that hijacked my otherwise capable brain and turned it into a kaleidoscope of Worst-Case Scenarios.

It doesn't matter how many "tools" Allen has given me for my "toolbox," every time it feels like the house is crumbling around me, I'd rather curl up in the fetal position than root around for a hammer. My unanxious brain can see things for what they are: sad or grueling or frightening, but not an imminent threat to my own safety. But my anxious brain knows that it *is* the rational brain, that these worries are not superficial when even a glance at the news app confirms that we are indeed living in the End of Times. Things are as bad as they seem, if not worse, and I'm worried that it was a mistake to have children, to bring them into the world when it feels like we're in the final act. On a road trip through northern Arizona, the sky is black with smoke from fires ripping through the high desert forests. We spend a summer break on a lake in Minnesota whose waters have receded so far that jumping off the dock would mean snapping your ankles on the lake bed that is just four inches below the surface of the water. Everything in our house will someday be a piece of garbage poisoning the earth. Allen asks me to practice interrupting the thought cycle: to see my thoughts floating in and decide whether or not I will think them. I'm not fast enough to be The Thought Catcher, and these ideas are slippery as minnows, though minnows are probably not long for this world, are they?

I've known since I can remember knowing anything that it's all going too fast, all spinning out of our control. Our parents proudly sent us to the Catholic grade school in our neighborhood, a three-story redbrick structure that loomed ominously over the local Walgreens we poured into after the bell rang, eager to buy two-for-a-dollar candy bars to split on the walk home. Catholic school conjures up a lot of assumptions: strict nuns, itchy uniforms, and daily Mass. But Annunciation Catholic School was different. We had uniforms and a few nuns, but we also had Mrs. Strickland.

Mrs. Strickland wore flowy dresses and jumpsuits, big silver rings on every finger, and an inordinate amount of authority for a woman whose one-woman department was Creative Arts. Creative Arts could and did mean anything. Twice a week, we'd walk to Mrs. Strickland's room, the former choir loft overlooking the former chapel was now our auditorium and lunchroom. There were no desks or chalkboards, no overhead lighting. Scarves covered the lamps, and a pile of cushions and carpet squares were our seats. The walls were covered with posters for Bob Dylan and the Grateful Dead, photos of past students and of Mrs. Strickland herself, younger but otherwise exactly the same, strumming an acoustic guitar on the stage below us. In our forty minutes together, she'd play music and we'd sing along, picking up lyrics as we went, unconcerned with tone, pitch, or harmony. We sang Joni Mitchell and Bob Dylan, "Free to Be You and Me," all songs we assumed she wrote herself. Once, Mrs. Strickland had cleared every classroom and arranged three-hundred-plus children in a circle in our auditorium to replicate the sounds of a rainstorm, pointing at us to indicate whether we should rub our hands together, snap our fingers, clap our hands, or stomp our feet. She played conductor for what felt like hours, and the rest of the teachers stood on the periphery, giving up on their lesson plans so that we could fully immerse ourselves in the creative art of . . . sound?

Other teachers were concerned with test scores and quizzes, but Mrs. Strickland was only concerned with our artistic expression . . . and hers. By the end of every September, our school schedules would revolve around the upcoming Christmas Pageant, a compulsory performance that included every student from kindergarten through eighth grade. Our school schedules would revolve around rehearsals and blockings and costume prep, Mrs. Strickland breezing into the math or science class to announce she needed us down in the auditorium to sing "Feliz Navidad." The Christmas Pageant included four nights of performances for parents and family, and matinee performances for the entire school, where we'd alternate from audience to performers in the same room where we ate our hot lunches and held our Girl Scout meetings. The pageant ended, every year, with over three hundred children singing Kermit's "The Christmas Wish," a song originally performed by an amphibious puppet that made our parents weep behind their camcorders. We understood our job in these performances was to evoke *feeling* in our audience, to impress upon our parents the fleeting nature of our childhoods and their lives. We knew that we had just these few years with Mrs. Strickland and with one another, that graduating from eighth grade would scatter us to different high schools and different futures, that we would one day be strangers to one another, names and faces in moldy yearbooks signed with bubble letters and scented pens. Mrs. Strickland's room was filled with the ephemera of kids who had come before us, some of whom were now the parents sitting in the auditorium, singing along to the same songs they had sung as children. We were nostalgic for childhoods that had not yet ended, already missing what was right in front of us.

Ralph is tall and reedy, with knobby knees and bony elbows. He weighs so little that if I lift him with too much enthusiasm, it feels like he could fly out of my arms and be carried away by a breeze. He is nearly five feet tall, and carrying him looks a little ridiculous, but every time he approaches me with his arms outstretched, I lift him up and feel his legs wrap around me. "Someday you won't be able to do this," he whispers into my hair, and I hold on a little bit tighter, knowing that the words that follow this sentence will be a pitch for a new video game or money for an in-app purchase, that this sentimentality is sincere and manipulative all at once. He has not had enough time to be seven, and I have not had enough time to hold him, none of it will ever be enough. At night, he asks me to sing to him, not caring about my lack of vocal range or whether I'm hitting the notes. I pull from my childhood and sing him the songs that Mrs. Strickland taught us. Some are silly—*sandwiches are beautiful, sandwiches are fine, I like sandwiches, I eat them all the time*—and some give me the same ache I had at his age. Bob Dylan's "Forever Young" hits a little different when you're singing it to your child than when you *are* a child.

My children are growing up spoiled and unappreciative of a world where the grown-ups in their lives appreciate and respect their feelings and mental health. They don't know that just a few decades ago, even adults dropped the r-word casually, and that words "mental" and "health" had yet to be paired together within the public consciousness. We certainly didn't refer to the unwell as "mentally ill" but by their specific diagnoses, real or assumed. People were nuts, schizo, bipolar, or fucking crazy. The absence of hearing voices or hallucinating indicated that you were A-OK, so what would you possibly have to complain about? Mrs. Strickland seemed to understand what so many adults did not: that childhood was uncertain and sometimes frightening, that the children she pulled out of math class to create an interpretive dance or to learn how to lip-synch Elton John already knew more about the world than we thought we did, that the passing of our childhood was no small thing, and that there was no such thing as a small event. Perspective is always relative, and while I can say with confidence that it is not the end of the world that our daughter is disliked by a classmate, it matters very much that it *feels* like the end of her world right now.

It all matters so much in the moment, no matter how old you are. The worries I'm tending to right now will someday disappear altogether, melted into the softest parts of my brain. I spent two years working with a (male) colleague who made my work and home life miserable. He was unkind on good days, cruel and punitive on bad ones. His name in my inbox filled me with dread, seeing him in a conference room pushed me into fight-or-flight. Writing this, I cannot for the life of me recall his name. Instead, he has been replaced with new nemeses and antagonists real and imagined. This will happen for our daughter, too. The girl who stares holes into the back of her skull in math class will be replaced by another person, and another, and another. Today's anxieties and shortcomings and grudges will be pushed to the edges of our consciousness, an endless spool of thread unraveling like I do every morning.

14

Asking for a Friend

If you text me and ask, "Can I vent to you?" The answer is going to be yes. I'll sit patiently at my phone watching those little dots pulse while you unload your personal thoughts onto your own screen. I'll validate you with emojis and words. I will gladly be the vessel for whatever it is you are carrying, and I will assure you that you are not strange or wrong or misreading things. Especially if what you want to vent about is your (lack of) friendships: how the friends you've had for years can't do anything but talk about their kids, or their partners, how none of them want to hang out anymore or when they do, they spend the entire time staring at their phones. How adulthood is lonelier than you ever thought it could be. Yes, it is. Many of us are sucked into the tornado of obligations and expectations, and we swirl past one another, shouting over the noise that "things should calm down any day now!" We text each other about how we really ought to get together soon, but looking at our calendars side by side we realize that the only free time we have in common is four a.m. on a Tuesday

127

sixteen months from now. Where we used to read each other's minds in a glance across a bar, we can't read the tone of this last text message . . . does she hate me? Is she mad at me?

Making friends as an adult is as brutal as losing them. The opportunities for a spontaneous bloom of connection are fewer and farther between, the risk of reaching out and being rejected much higher than when there was a class-room of other options around you. As a parent, most of the new adults you meet are the parents of your children's friends, and there's no telling what kind of tree the apple fell from when your only source of information is four years old and doesn't *know* where Lindleigh's parents stand on LGBTQ issues, or climate change. There's an (accurate) saying about midwesterners: they met all the friends they'll ever need in high school. They'll stay friends forever, and even if you're a perfectly friendly co-worker, you're going to be held at arm's length because they've only got so many seats at the table for couples game night, nothing personal! It's not my experience personally, because I met my oldest friends when I was in second grade. My family had moved back to South Minneapolis after a few years in rural Minnesota, and I was going to a new Catholic school. Crucifixion, where I'd gone for kindergarten and first grade, was vastly different from Annunciation. While the name was more intense, the living was easier: Crucifixion didn't have school uniforms, and lunch was served by a group of old ladies who cooked every meal themselves. We went to Mass every day, which was a drag, but because we were too young to have received any sacraments, we were there just to fill the pews and look cute.

The kids at Annunciation wore uniforms and packed their

own lunches, a combination that felt chaotic: our daily outfits were decided for us, but lunch was a free-for-all? And it *was* chaotic. On my first day of school, a bespectacled girl named Amy Ruff stood up and declared her small carton of chocolate milk "up for grabs" before sitting down and shouting, "down for keeps!" She did this over and over, delighting everyone at the table except me. Up for *grabs*? Down for *keeps*? What kind of madness was this? I sat silently through lunch and gym and social studies, my loneliness sitting like a hot coal in the center of my chest. At Crucifixion, I'd have spent the lunch hour eating mashed potatoes next to my best friend, Allie, then heading outside for a game of tag. Instead, I tried to choke down bites of the sticky peanut butter and jelly sandwich my mother had packed for me, then stepped out onto the playground alone, willing myself to disappear entirely.

At Annunciation, Erin and Cara were a pair, best friends since kindergarten. They walked each other home after school and joined the same park board sports teams and wore their hair in the same puffy shoulder-length cut, their natural curls brushed out into waves. On Twin Day—a day when you didn't have to wear a uniform but *did* have to find a classmate to dress like you—they were always each other's twin, with matching outfits *and* shoes. Our class was only forty-eight kids split into two classrooms, so it shouldn't have taken three years for us to become friends, but it did. I lived on the wrong side of Lyndale Avenue, and our paths home went in opposite directions until my parents bought a house on Humboldt Avenue and Erin, Cara, and I were stuck at the same crosswalk after school. Eventually, we went from crossing the street together to walking to Erin's house after school, where her mother, Jan, would have a pitcher of Kool-Aid and a freezer full of appetizers ready to thaw for us. We were a throuple, and as everyone knows, three is the perfect number that always means nobody at all is left out. Like every young friendship, there was a certain amount of misery: the abuse of three-way calling that every landline-using millennial used to Judas one another by sitting silently on the line while one friend cajoled another into talking shit about you; overlapping crushes that left us angry at each other but never at the boy, etc. etc. All of those rifts were easily mended by our proximity and our shared history. Eventually, the icy silence would melt and we'd all be in the back seat of our friend Gene's car, driving around the Minneapolis lakes with Big Gulps of Diet Coke and a mix CD blasting through the tinny speakers of his 1988 Mazda MX-6. With Gene, we were a four-pack. A complete unit.

Erin and Cara and Gene I went to high school together, and college apart. We spent our holiday breaks sitting in our parents' living rooms and meeting up in shitty bars. When we graduated, we flew to one another's cities for long weekends, sleeping three to a bed like we were still in middle school. Gene always said he was fine on the floor, like a good boy. We planned one another's wedding showers and baby showers, got pregnant at around the same time, and planned for our children to maintain the next generation of this friendship.

And then Aaron died.

What nobody wants to say about grieving people is this: they are the worst. I believe a kinder aphorism is that hurt people hurt people. It is most likely unintentional, though that doesn't make it sting any less when you're on the receiving end of a person's misplaced pain. But an emotionally destroyed person, a person who struggles to maintain any level of self-love, will also find it hard to maintain relationships. And being friends with Erin and Cara was hard. Their husbands were young and healthy and alive. They could and did pick up their own crying children, pick up milk on their way back from work, pick the movie on Friday nights. And I was on my own, a one-woman show trying to raise a small child and not get my sad all over him. It was all I could think about, and nothing I could talk about. It was a lot for me, and I assumed too much for anyone else. I ran to Erin when Aaron died. Ralph and I booked one-way tickets to any city where we had friends with a guest room, and Erin and her husband, Kris, and their daughter, Emma, lived in a two-bedroom in San Francisco, just a few blocks from the Embarcadero. Ralph and I stayed in the full-size bed they kept for guests, next to Emma's crib. Ralph and Emma are just a few months apart, and Erin was pregnant with her second baby. I'd lost my second pregnancy six weeks before Aaron died, and every so often Ralph would remember that we'd told him he had a sibling coming. "Where's *my* baby?" he'd ask in his little elfin voice, and I would offer him an incomprehensible explanation and another bowl of apple sauce. I had no job and nowhere to be, and Erin and I spent days walking our kids around the city in their all-terrain strollers, pushing them on swings. We ate sourdough bread bowls at Boudin and put the kids down for naps in the same crib, then Erin would look at me with her glowing brown eyes and ask me how I was doing and I would look at her and tell her anything but the truth, and she would pretend to believe me. At night, Kris would come home from work and get dinner started. He'd bounce Emma on his knee and Ralph would hug his legs and I would watch the moment like I was a child staring into a snow globe, wishing I could live inside it.

Cara is the group historian. There is not a single moment of our shared childhood or adolescence that she cannot recall with clarity.

What color was my homecoming dress sophomore year?

Which teacher threw a textbook at a kid and broke the black-board?

What was the name of the guy I hooked up with on a Grey-hound bus?

Whatever the question, Cara remembers the answer, and additional details you may have also forgotten. For decades, even our personal experiences were shared: we *all* took the ACT, went to college, got jobs and fell in and out of love. But none of them had cremated their spouse. None of them had watched their partner die. Only I had crossed the imaginary threshold between the world they lived in and the world I now inhabited. These losses often felt like a thick plate of glass that separated me from the rest of the world, like I was watching everyone from a distance, unable to connect.

Childhood friendships end declaratively. My youngest son will come home from preschool with a full report of who is or is not currently his friend: Benjamin and Iris? Friends. Victor? Depends on the day. There isn't a lot of drama to it, just a shifting of the relational abacus. Adolescent friendships end by taking a match to every bridge connecting you: gifts are discarded, notes are burned, phone numbers and handles are blocked. Most of us are given no training for maintaining or ending or healing interpersonal relationships in adulthood, romantic or platonic. After Aaron died, I didn't return texts and I didn't confirm plans. I forgot about birthdays and I stopped returning calls. I didn't know how to show up for them: the Nora they had known before was gone, and I didn't like this version of me enough to show her to anyone who had known and loved those better versions. I assumed that their lives were perfectly fine without me, and they assumed I didn't need them, and we let the current of assumptions pull us apart until I was exactly as alone as I feared I would be. The crush of adulthood flooded into the space left between us; packed calendars of kids' sports and work presentations and thirty minutes of cardio a day to keep our metabolisms humming along, and soon I didn't know any more about the current state of my friends' lives than any stranger on social media would have been able to surmise. These relationships hadn't ended, they had just slipped into a liminal space between friends and acquaintances.

As Christians on social media say, "People come into your life for a reason or a season." There are only four seasons to the calendar year, but in the life of a Christian woman? Oh man, the seasons are endless and ever-changing! Perhaps it would be easier to live this phrase, that people are here for a purpose or for a specific amount of time (I concede the idea is improved with a rhyme), if we weren't subjected to a constant window into each other's lives in perpetuity. Decades ago, a former friend would fade into the background of your memory, brought to the forefront if you saw them in the dairy aisle while running errands or if someone asked, "Whatever happened to so-and-so, you used to be so close?" Social media keeps a superficial but quite real connection to people we are no longer connected with. You can see someone's Thanksgiving table, their child's first day of school, and their anniversary message to their partner without ever speaking to them. You're informed, sure, but are you connected? And what does that information do for you? Do to you? When the threads connecting you have been stretched thin, when do you decide to cut them altogether? Anyone would suggest you unfollow a former partner to protect your peace of mind, but unfollowing a friend feels rude or petty and so permanent: a declaration that the relationship is no longer what it was, and that it never will be.

I've made and lost plenty of friends over the years, because that rhyme is accurate: not every relationship is forever. A few of them are sworn enemies whose names fill me with hot rage, but most of these relationships just fizzled or faded. There was no falling out; no tearful, drunken rant like you'd expect after being a regular viewer of Real Housewives for years; just enough distance that you'd forget they exist, until you run into them again. That's not what I want, and I know it. And it's not like Erin and Cara and I aren't *friends*, we see each other over Christmas and once a summer, and we fall into the same banter we always have. But I don't want to be the friendship equivalent of a booty call, I want to know how their workday was and what their plans are for the weekend; I want to know what they're watching on Netflix and what kind of mascara they prefer. I want to be the person they call when they have five extra minutes to talk, and I know that I'm not.

But how do you reach out when months and months have passed, when Christmas cards have arrived but you haven't had a meaningful conversation in years? So awkward. It had been years since we'd exchanged more than a few text messages and a casual meetup with our children in tow, so long since we'd cracked the surface. But someone had to make the first move, so I wrote the texts and I made the calls and I did the most painful thing: acknowledge the pain I caused and the pain I felt, and hoped there would still be room for me.

Thirty years after that first day of school, when I watched Erin and Cara practicing one-armed cartwheels together on the blacktop, the three of us have convened for a long weekend in Vail, Colorado. It's been a few months since I started to actually *be* a friend, and the reignited text thread had us all confessing that we are on the edge, that we needed some time and space away from our families and obligations, and fast. Erin is sure that something is wrong with her youngest child—at a year old, he's not yet walking or talking—and Cara and I are sure that she is wrong, and he is perfect. We meet at Erin's house and hold him and marvel at him, assure her that he is better than fine and that every baby is different, moves at their own pace. Ralph, I remind her, didn't walk until he was nineteen months old and a physical therapist at the children's hospital diagnosed him with an unusually large head that made it hard for him to balance.

But Erin is a pediatric nurse, and her experience and her gut tell her it is something else. Something isn't right, she insists. We leave Erin's house in Denver three hours later than we expected, but once we hit the highway, we've hit our stride. Erin has a playlist of our favorite songs from the past few decades, but almost immediately we've turned the music down because there's just so much to talk about. The highway winds its way into mountains so large that it makes the Phoenix mountains look like slight hills, our ears pop with the elevation and as the miles disappear beneath the wheels of Erin's SUV, the distance between us closes. Our conversation weaves through the past and the future, layering in our shared and individual memories, coloring in the blank spaces, leaning on Cara to fact-check the details for us.

The pool is closed by the time we finally arrive, but the boy at the front desk must have seen enough middle-aged mothers come through this lobby to decipher the looks on our faces. He tells us that if we're quiet enough nobody will complain, and he probably won't even notice. I use my long arms to unlock the gate from the inside, and we swim under the summer stars, the way we'd swim in Lake Harriet at night when we were in high school, even though the duck-infested waters gave us a rash. When we're finished, we sit cross-legged on the couch and talk the way we did as middle schoolers, laughing so hard I'm sure that Jan Mulcahy will come down the stairs and tell us to quiet down and get some sleep.

I didn't just miss these women, I missed *out* on these women, these women who used to be the girls who saved me a seat on the bus and shared their lunches with me during my many growth spurts where the *two* brown-bag lunches my mother packed for me weren't enough. These women I envied for their living husbands and their beautiful homes, the pregnancies they brought to term—they too had been struggling and suffering these past few years. We weep and we weep, aghast at the pain we've each been carrying inside, relieved to have it spill out, honored to share this space together again and aware of how easy it would be to let it slip away.

Months later, Erin calls me. Sophie and I are about to get our nails done and have just unbuckled our seat belts when my phone rings. Erin was right about her baby, and the two of us weep on the phone while we try to make sense of what is happening.

"I love you, and I'm here," I say to her, and I can hear her nodding her head.

Minutes later, Cara calls, and together we hold the pieces of our friend's broken heart.

The three of us were Girl Scouts for just a few years. It was fun to make crafts after school, but less fun to stand outside of a Walgreen's in the freezing cold trying to convince adults to buy cookies from a group of strange little girls who could take cash or check. We dropped out by fifth grade, but I can still remember holding hands with our troop mates and singing:

"A circle is round, it has no end.
That's how long, I will be your friend."

15

Bad Bosses

Work-life balance had not yet been invented when I started my career. Millennials had a bad rap before we'd even entered the workforce—we were needy and entitled and lazy long before we even opened our matching 401(k) plans—and everyone I knew seemed desperate to prove our detractors wrong. My friends and I all happily logged into our email addresses from our crappy little apartments, checking in after hours from the used sofas where we watched *The Hills* and *Rock of Love*, using the laptops we'd bought in college. We competed to be the first to arrive at the office and the last to leave, marking our productivity by the time spent in the office, hunched over spreadsheets and PowerPoint presentations. Drunk on the elixir of new adulthood—the sheer thrill of having responsibilities like bills to pay and grocery shopping to do on our own—we happily dissolved all boundaries between work and home. I was envious of Lauren, whose position as an assistant account executive at a large New York

City advertising agency had come with a BlackBerry, a digital leash to make sure she was never "out of pocket" for clients or superiors. Hearing it buzz, she'd rush to where it sat on the dingy coffee table, cluttered with bottles of nail polish and old magazines, tapping away at the tiny QWERTY keyboard with her thumbs. "Just putting out a fire," she'd sigh, and I'd swoon internally, imagining a world where the fate of *anything* rested in my thumbs. Even the media we loved mirrored our experiences. Just a few weeks before the power went out, I'd gone to see *The Devil Wears Prada* with a friend who worked as a New York City schoolteacher. I'd shivered in recognition as Andy, the protagonist, struggled with her demanding boss. We all screamed at the TV when Lauren Conrad declined the trip to Paris at her summer internship at *Teen Vogue* on *The Hills*, choosing instead to spend the summer with her greasy boyfriend, Jason. It felt strange to side with her boss, but Lisa Love was right when she looked down her elegant nose and said the iconic line, "You'll always be the girl who didn't go to Paris."

My boss, who we'll call Freya, was the Great Hope of our company. Unlike the rest of us midwestern hillbillies without taste or sophistication, Freya was a real New Yorker with real connections. Rumors about her flew through our email server from other entry-level employees who worked in our midwestern offices. They claimed she traveled with an extra seat just for her Rolodex, that she thought she was *better than us*, that she looked down on everyone outside of the New York office. They were right about the last two points, but Freya never tried to hide it. On conference calls, where I sat silently typing out notes that would need to be emailed to every meeting attendee within thirty minutes of the call, she would mute the phone and cackle at the ideas of our midwestern colleagues. She wore her hair in a dark bob and dressed in clothes that I learned to identify as expensive, authentic versions of the dresses and shoes and shirts and bags I bought at Target and Old Navy. She lived in the East Village, and her two daughters went to school with several famous people whose names were always whispered, like they might be lurking around the next cubicle. She'd been a magazine editor "in a previous life," as she liked to say, and this gave her extra authority in our organization.

Freya talked about New York City the way upperclassmen in college talked about the school you attended in common; like it had once been different, better . . . before you came along, of course. "I don't know that I've ever even *been* to Queens," she'd say when I talked about my neighborhood, where the pizza guy always gave me an extra slice if I left my boyfriend out on the sidewalk, and where our dinners "out" were from the hot dog stand that also sold papaya juice. I feared and admired Freya, who either spoke down to me or spoke to me like I was also a woman of taste and style, a person who could appreciate a new handbag that cost more than I made in a month or who could identify a quality towel beyond "this one doesn't smell like mildew." Freya pronounced the word "croissant" as *cwah-sahn* and only drank cappuccinos and was always on a diet. Hers was the literal corner office next to my tan-and-gray cubicle, and I thrilled and shuddered at the sound of my name being screamed from her desk, where she'd squawk that she didn't have a delete button, or that the document she'd spent all day on had evaporated before her eyes. My true value as a millennial was proven by my ability to navigate simple word-processing programs and connect to our printer.

Freya had her own assistant, an entire person whose job it was to order her lunch and pick up her coffee and book and decline meetings, but I was happy to pick up any remaining tasks that would gain me more approval. There was nothing Freya could ask me to do—stand in line for Shake Shack for hours because she had a craving, dump the contents of her handbag on the floor to find a missing lipstick, take her anorexic daughter out for pizza in hopes that she'd be cured by watching "a girl like me" house a slice—that I wouldn't say yes to. My boyfriend at the time was also my roommate. He worked for the city of New York, filling out reports and time cards, filing for overtime when he went over forty hours per week. My work life did not compute for him. Why exactly was I staying at the office until seven p.m.? Why was I checking my email on a Saturday morning? I told him that he didn't understand, which was correct. He *didn't* understand. His boss wouldn't allow them to work overtime without approval, because overtime was compensated. He took his lunch hour every day, away from the office. He did not know what kind of underwear his boss preferred, or where she lived. He certainly had not been inside that home, had not seen where she and her husband slept and ate and watched TV. His work lived at work, and mine followed me around. I didn't have a BlackBerry, but I kept my email open on my laptop all night, replying to every question that Freya lobbed my way, usually all crammed in the subject line:

Bad Bosses

EMERGENCY: *ELLE DECOR NEEDS A SAMPLE COURIERED FIRST THING TOMORROW WHERE IS OUR PRESS REPORT FOR APRIL???? IS THERE WATER IN THE FRIDGE?????*

And when she asked if I could babysit her daughter's hamster while they went to their country house upstate? I said yes, and I added an extra hour onto my evening commute, walking through the sweltering heat from Union Square to the East Village to feed and water a small rodent, then taking several trains back up to Queens. I was heartened by the (implied) promise that when my ordeal was over, I'd be richer. The parents I often babysat for, whose children went to a fancy private school with Freya's children, paid me twenty dollars an hour to babysit their children, tacking on an extra forty dollars or so to pay for cabs that I never took, pocketing the money and taking the subway home. Surely spending two weeks taking care of a hamster would bring me some extra cash. I had already spent it in my mind on Dunkin Donuts iced coffees and a trip to the movies, where I'd shiver in the cold of the theater.

When Saturday came around, I woke up in a thick sweat and made my pilgrimage to tend to The Hamster. Everything in the apartment was as I'd left it; I added their mail to the pile on the dining table and walked into the kids' bedroom where The Hamster (did he have a name??) lived in a small plastic cage on top of a desk.

He wasn't there.

I lifted up the small igloo-like piece of molded plastic where he liked to nap: no hamster. I ran my fingers through the wood shavings, hoping he had burrowed in for a nap: no hamster. I retraced my footsteps from the day before: I'd fed him his pellets, held him until he bit me, and then put him back in his cage, securing the gate as always. So where. The hell. Was. The. Hamster?!?!

I checked behind every piece of furniture and under every cushion. I grabbed a carrot from the crisper drawer and set it in the middle of the living room floor, waiting with my legs curled up on the couch for him to emerge from whatever hidey-hole he was napping in and take the bait. He did not show his face, and I was stricken. I had one job: keep the hamster alive. That he would also remain within their family home was a nonverbal expectation, but I imagined they would not be happy to hear that their beloved pet was missing in action. I was done for. I briefly considered stopping into a pet store to see if I could find a convincing replacement, but decided that honesty was the best policy, a decision I would come to regret. Freya's husband answered her phone, and I heard the words pouring out of me, out of order and far too quickly. When I was done talking, there was just silence. "Well," he said with a sigh, and my heart unclenched, "this is incredibly disappointing. I don't even know what to say."

I didn't either, and so I said nothing, afraid that the cry stuck in my throat would escape.

"You know," he continued, "you can't just play with a hamster and not lock the cage when you're done."

My eyes narrowed. *Play* with the hamster? I was a twenty-four-year-old adult woman being taken advantage of, not a child practicing wish fulfillment by dropping by to play dolls with a little mammal! I mumbled an apology and hung up the phone, a bloom of anxiety flowering in my stomach.

Freya barely looked at me when she walked back into the office. She never paid me for the time I had spent schlepping back and forth from Queens to the East Village. I started looking for jobs. The Devil did sometimes wear Prada (or at least a Chinatown knockoff backpack—I couldn't tell the difference), and I was always going to be the girl who lost The Hamster.

My interview was a scant six blocks from my current office, which meant I only had to make a big deal out of *casually* leaving the office for lunch, taking great pains to let Freya know that today I was *going out to lunch* instead of eating a free bagel from the communal table while huddling over my keyboard. Why was I wearing an actual outfit instead of a free T-shirt from my college days? Oh, just trying to change it up a bit! I speed-walked up Fifth Avenue and into the cool lobby of a building that sat right on Madison Square Park.

Bethany met me at the door of the office wearing a neat, rich-lady bob and those rich-lady slippers embroidered with something dumb like teddy bears. People pay hundreds of dollars for these shoes, and like many things that rich people love, they are ugly. Bethany settled into her desk and motioned for me to sit in the chair facing her. Behind her loomed an eight-foot portrait, a photo of a woman in a ball gown taken in what looked like the '80s, her hair blowing in the imaginary inside wind. I assumed it was a portrait of the designer Donna Karan, that this woman was a fan. She noticed me noticing

it and smiled. "Beautiful, isn't it? I *wish* I was still that thin."
She had the boniness of a hungry bird.

To kick off the interview, Bethany handed me a pen
and paper and asked me to draw what I was looking for in
a career. The friend who'd recruited me to the position had
warned me that this might happen, and so I tried not to look
at the portrait that was staring down at me, and drew what I
thought Bethany would want to see: a ladder (for climbing),
hands holding each other (for friendship), a mountain (also
for climbing, but in this case representing challenges), and
a smiley face (for happiness, duh). I did not include a draw-
ing of an insurance card or a dollar sign. Bethany seemed
very excited to know that I had grown up in the Midwest.
Was my father a farmer, she asked? I joked that he was actually Paul Bunyan, and not knowing the reference to a mythi-
cal giant lumberjack, she told me she could tell I came from
good stock.

My first day on the job, Emily was assigned to show me
the ropes. Emily had big, white teeth; red hair straightened
to a blunt lob; and tan, freckled skin. I could have gotten the
lay of the land by simply turning my body 360 degrees while
standing at my desk: the office was on open space filled with
gray cubicles. Windows to the outside were monopolized by
the three offices: Bethany's, which took up nearly one-third
of the total office space and adjoined the conference room,
and two small spaces for our managers, which were roughly
the size of a cubicle, but with closing doors. Instead, Emily
walked me around the cubicles, introducing me to more and
more beautiful girls. Emily showed me the fax machine, whispering that because my desk was closest to it, I *had* to make

sure there was always enough paper in it. "Bethany is *really* concerned about paper in the fax machine," she said as neutrally as possible, a tone which I grew to understand meant, "You have signed a deal with the devil and it's too late to back down now." Next to the fax machine there was a small fridge, which Emily explained should never hold an open beverage or any food more than a day old, and a microwave that should never be left "with time on it." I was confused about the microwave part. What did she mean "with time on it?" Emily lowered her voice, "If you put something in for a minute, and you take it out with seventeen seconds remaining, you *need* to press clear. Bethany does *not like to see time left on the microwave. She thinks it can cause an explosion.*" I nodded as though I'd applied for a job managing small household appliances.

Our alleged job at this agency was to provide public relations counsel for luxury brands, and I was a girl who couldn't identify a pair of the most popular designer flats of the era, now writing press releases for a developer of luxury homes in the ten- to thirty-million-dollar range. The "luxury brands" mission was more aspirational than reality; most of our clients were brands you've never heard of unless you're an enthusiastic reader of Crock-Pot recipe books. Going to work was the closest I've ever been to a sorority: the only men we worked with were clients or air-conditioner repairmen, and we took our lunches out to the park whenever the weather was nice enough. Kristen was right: the pay was *great*. My salary jumped 30 percent just by joining Bethany's agency, and she regularly treated us to champagne happy hours or lunches at restaurants we'd never be able to afford on our own. Bethany *loved* us. She told us all about her lonely childhood growing up on Central Park West with only a nanny to take care of her. She told us all about her ghoulish first husband and her dashing second husband, whose betrayal had her standing in the middle of Fifth Avenue traffic in her nightgown, out of her mind with grief. And occasionally her "darling third husband" would make an appearance at our office, stepping in to take her to lunch. He was seemingly charmed by all of her quirks, which included tipping cabdrivers only by rounding up to the next dollar, shouting to the cleaning staff to "TAKE THE BASURA! THE BASURA," as if they didn't know how to identify a trash can. Bethany wore a floor-length fur coat the moment the weather dropped below fifty, and shouted to every man who walked into the office—whether they were there as a client or to fix the AC—"These are my beautiful girls!," introducing us one by one by what she saw as our defining characteristic, like the Real Housewives of an Office. I was a midwesterner with a "good work ethic" (Was I?), Emily and Kristen were "fiery redheads," and our intern Denise was a "glamour-puss," which is uncomfortable to type and uncomfortable to hear said aloud.

Every week, Bethany would announce that she was going to the bank and sweep out of the office for several hours. When she returned, she'd sit at her desk and start calling people in. I'd watch from my back cubicle as my colleagues stepped into her office and closed the door behind them, and we'd all started messaging each other immediately, speculating on what was happening. The subject would casually return to her desk and begin reporting back: Bethany had given them a reprimand, or a raise, or approved their request for vacation time.

Bad Bosses

It turned out, Bethany's trips to the bank were actually trips to her therapist, a mysterious man named Ike who gave Bethany a lot of work advice. "Wait 'til you meet Ike," Emily said one day. "He's a trip." I didn't ask any of the obvious questions, like "Why would I meet my boss's therapist" or "Why do *you* know our boss's therapist?" Instead I laughed along, not wanting to find myself in another "I just assumed your shoes were also from Payless" kind of moment. Emily knew Ike because she'd been to dinner with him. So had the other two managers. The three of them—a leadership team of women under thirty—went to dinner with Ike regularly. He'd make a reservation at someplace fancy and expensive—Le Cirque, Country, Craft Steak—all names I knew from booking dinners for my previous boss, and the four of them would eat and drink and talk about work . . . and about Bethany. The next day, when Bethany "went to the bank," she was really meeting with Ike. Her return to the office, and whatever happened afterward, seemed to be a direct result of those meetings. We all learned that if you needed something, you had to get to Ike.

I needed Bethany to stop editing my emails. Before I was able to reply to any client email—even one as simple as "Yep!"—she'd ask to see my reply. Sometimes she'd stand behind me as I typed "Yep!" And offer some light edits until the email was now this:

Dear Margene,
Thank you for your email; it was, as always, a true
delight to see your name appear in my inbox. Per your
request, the information you inquired after will be
available to me by 12 pm EST today. I will certainly

149

keep you apprised and will reply to you as soon as I have confirmation.

Please, as always, do not hesitate to contact me with any further questions.

All best,

Nora

All Best was a required sign-off, one I'd never seen before or since. I'd seen *best* and *all the best*, but never *all best*. Often, Bethany asked me to print out a draft of my reply, which she would line edit with red pen and then return to me, standing behind me as I retyped the email and pressed send under her watchful eye. This process meant that it often took hours to reply to clients who just wanted to know whether or not the meeting was indeed scheduled. I bitched about this to my colleagues over lunch and after-work drinks, and I wasn't the only one. She was asking all of us to print and edit our emails, which seemed inefficient at best. Didn't our clients notice that all the young women they worked with had suddenly morphed into rich older women? Weren't they confused as to why we wrote "all best" when it truly didn't make any sense? Weeks after we had all agreed that email edits were simply too much, a verdict was reached: we needed an Ike dinner.

Ike was smaller than I thought he'd be, with a warm face that reminded me of a chipmunk (that is absolutely a compliment; chipmunks are some of the cutest little mammals ever). He was tan, with a bright smile, and when he swanned up to our table, he hugged and kissed all the girls he had met before. He grabbed his menu and ordered bottles of wine for the table, relieving us of the pressure to know what to order at a restaurant whose entrees represented more than a day's worth of take-home pay. We'd stopped at a bar for drinks on the way, Emily slamming down her company AMEX and announcing, "This one's on Bethany!" The entire dinner was on Bethany, it turns out, and as we were subsisting mostly on reheated pasta with butter and the occasional salad from the takeout place on Twenty-Eighth and Broadway, we went big. In between bites and rounds of wine, Ike asked us about ourselves and our work, and reassured us that we were not alone. All his clients—major, high-profile people, he reminded us—had these same problems, even Gwyneth! It seemed strange that he'd drop client names—actors and professional baseball players—and stranger still that Gwyneth Paltrow was also struggling with her boss asking her to print her emails? It all seemed odd, but he was a mental health professional, wasn't he? This was his job! To listen to our problems and help us fix them! He offered no advice or insight, and took no notes. At the end of the night, Ike handed the bill to Emily. We took cabs or black cars home to our shitty apartments and woke up hungover.

And it worked.

The next day, after her "trip to the bank," Bethany told me to "go ahead and reply to Margene, I don't need to see it!" She called this out from behind her desk as though it were the most natural thing in the world, as though we hadn't spent thirty minutes the previous day wrestling over the exact wording to inform that client that no, Oprah would *not* be including their Crock-Pot Christmas recipe book in her favorite things roundup.

My roommates found these dinners to be alarming. "You're

going to dinner? With your boss's shrink? *Without* her?" Well, when you say it like that, of course it seems strange. And it was strange, but it was also strangely delightful. I went to restaurants I could never afford, I was seen and heard by a mental health professional, and I always, always got what I wanted afterward. Yes, it was a little uncomfortable when he invited us all to his home in the Hamptons for a party, but no big deal, I just didn't go. What my normie roommates didn't understand was that Ike was a cheat code between us and what we wanted: vacation time, a raise, the basic dignity of not being scolded for letting the fax machine paper dwindle to under fifty individual sheets of paper for an already outdated mode of communication. Dinner guests varied: extreme issues (a promotion or an impending resignation) might earn you a one-on-one, interpersonal conflict would involve the aggrieved parties, and the best dinners included the entire office . . . minus Bethany. We always got drinks beforehand, and we always got way too drunk during dinner. We were young and dazzled by the elegance of it all: that our boss had a therapist who wanted to wine us, dine us, and let us whine while dining? It was too much to resist. At least, for a while.

Two years after that first day, nearly all of us had moved on to new jobs. The energy at the office had gone from quirky to questionable: Bethany had closed-circuit television cameras installed in the four corners of our open office, which she watched on her computer monitor. She became convinced that our cleaning person was going to try to break into the office, and more convinced that we were all going to leave her. She didn't have to read our emails anymore, but she was always watching us, always pulling us into her office and closing the door, asking us what we *really thought* of our colleagues. Was Christy phoning it in? Was Allie a "good fit"? Ike dinners and Ike lunches became more frequent and less about fun and food and more about strategic alliances and betrayals that seemed to be orchestrated by Ike and Bethany. I'd experience panic attacks so intense I was sure I was dying, and migraines so strong that my vision would blur. When I put in my notice—strategically timed about ten minutes before leaving town for my grandmother's funeral—she called my parents and urged them to urge me to reconsider. Many jobs later, Ike Dinners were nothing but an anecdote.

Having a bad boss is terrible, and so is *being* a boss in general. Management books and HR trainings all exist in a hypothetical world where clients don't assume that your workday continues until eleven p.m., and where the general public doesn't demand instantaneous solutions to mild problems. For all the shit I talked about my own bosses, I myself am a horrible boss. I've behaved like Freya and Bethany and many of the other deeply unstable, very demanding people who have been in charge of my career. I've been vague in my directions, harsh with criticism and slow to give credit, and more than once I've asked for coffee "the color of a brown paper bag." I know very few people who are suited for tending to the professional growth and satisfaction of other people, who thrive in making sure people are productive but not burned out, that they're meeting or exceeding expectations while also trying to meet or exceed the expectations set by their own bosses. Knowing that other people's ability to pay their bills hinges on your ability to keep a company going, requires a kind of mental fortitude I learned the hard way that I do not have. I'm not built to be the boss of anyone, including myself, who I tend to micromanage and verbally abuse. Today, I'm bravely breaking the cycle by refusing to be in charge of anyone or anything.

As we get older, we start to see our parents as *people:* flawed individuals who did their best with what they had. We start to understand that some of our worst habits and behaviors were inherited, like our double-jointed thumbs or "strong noses," but that with awareness, we can break the cycle of whatever generational trauma is haunting our lineage. Doesn't this hold true professionally, to an extent? Aren't we all a product of the generational work trauma experienced by our bosses, their bosses, all the way back to the very first boss? Aren't all of us except Jeff Bezos and Elon Musk and the Koch Brothers and maybe, like, two other guys just cogs in a machine that was built and set in motion long before we had a corporate email address?

Bethany and Freya did not spring into the world fully formed like modern-day corporate Athenas. They came of professional age in a time where your male colleague grabbing your ass was called a "regular Tuesday," and where the glass ceiling kicked in at the second floor. The rumors that swirled around Freya in our company weren't about her professional capabilities, they were about *her.* And yes, she crossed several boundaries during our short time together, but had she ever been allowed any boundaries herself? Yes, she once took me aside after a meeting and told me that I should *turn off my personality* for clients and yes, that created in me a deep insecurity that has followed me for decades, but maybe she was just trying to teach me how to survive in the world she'd mastered, one where her own personality was blunted and reshaped to fit whatever was needed of her in the moment.

Even Bethany isn't simply a villain, but also a victim. In 2019, Ike was the subject of a podcast called *The Shrink Next Door*, which exposed him for manipulating his clients into hiring him as a business consultant, where he gave them advice on hiring, firing, and managing employees, and in more than one case had them rewrite their wills to include *him*. I don't know how long Bethany's relationship with Ike lasted, or how deep it went, but I know that she trusted this man, too.

I've lost touch with these women over the years, but I'm sure they have their own version of these stories, just as valid as mine. I'm grateful to them both for the stories and the paychecks, for the letters of recommendation and for letting me take home the conference room bagels. And wherever they are, I sincerely wish them *All Best. . . .*

16

Anything Can Happen

My family lore includes many almosts; brushes with death that we children just narrowly escaped. As a toddler, our cousin Lillian wandered out her front door and walked several city blocks, unattended, after misunderstanding her mother's directive to go next door to ask for a cup of sugar. Our youngest brother, Patrick, stood up in his crib and reached the cord for the plastic venetian blinds in his bedroom window. He'd secured them around his neck and was in the process of strangling himself when our older brother— just nine years old—walked in and calmly untangled him. Our cousin Phil fell into the fire pit at our cabin and once again our oldest brother pulled him out before the flames could catch the synthetic fibers of his sweatpants. During a family trip to Italy for a wedding, my father drove us through the winding switchbacks in the hills of Tuscany, on the way to our rental home on an olive grove. The car was a minivan with a manual transmission that ran on diesel fuel, and on the one-lane roads my father required complete silence. These unpaved roadways were originally intended for one mule, and then a tiny car, and meeting a vehicle coming the opposite direction meant one of you had to reverse until there was a small rest area next to the road. I sat in the back seat averting my eyes from the window and listening to James Taylor's *Greatest Hits* or Britney Spears's first album on my CD player, which was not as skip-free as it had been advertised. And then, the back wheel of our van slipped off the soft shoulder of the road and our car slid over the edge of a small mountain, pressing me against the window, my unbuckled brother and grandmother on top of me as we started to plummet to our deaths before stopping suddenly. Two small trees—one at each axel—were all that suspended us perpendicular to the road above. If you've seen any movies at all, you know that any movement as small as a cough could cause the weight of a car to shift, and so we did not speak at all. My brain prepared a last thought: *Does everyone know how much you love them?* And then it shut off, while all of us moved in silent, sloth-like precision to manually roll down the windows and crawl out, first my mother from the passenger side, and then my father. Together, they lifted the heavy door to pull out our grandmother, who had just graduated college in her mid-eighties and had her whole life ahead of her, and then my little brother, a high school freshman. And then the door slammed shut, and the car shuddered, and I prepared myself for death. But in a wild turn of events that you definitely would not see coming, I did not die. I crawled out of the open window after saving the gold necklace I had bought for my high school boyfriend, and lay panting on the dirt road, clinging to it as if it hadn't just betrayed all of us.

Anything Can Happen

"Did you have a last thought?" I asked my dad, and he stared straight ahead, nodding.

"Steve, you just killed your whole family."

It seemed like a bad time to remind him that he had two other children back in the United States who had not been invited on this trip.

Our uncle Maurice was two years old when he toed the line between this world and the next. It was spring in Minneapolis, a season of false starts and fake outs. The sun was strong enough to melt the snow, but not strong enough to warm the air, and my uncle was in the front yard, bundled in his woolen snowsuit. The house was a small craftsman bungalow just a block from Minnehaha Creek, which winds through the city before joining the Mighty Mississippi less than a mile from my grandparents' home. Grandma Viv had left Maurice under the authoritative eye of his five-year-old sister while she ran up to the hardware store her father owned. When she returned, a neighbor from a block away was sitting on the front stoop with her son, who was soaking wet. Maurice had walked across Forty-Sixth Street and directly into the creek, where he'd been swept away by the rushing waters. The wool of his snowsuit had kept him afloat, and two women out for a spring stroll happened to be crossing a footbridge as he floated by. They screamed, and a neighbor who was out tending to his winter-browned lawn sprinted to the rescue. The Minneapolis *Star and Tribune* reported on the story, calling it a miracle. As a person who believes in God but cannot commit to a religion, "miracle" is a lovely word and an inadequate one. Who doles out these miracles, and how? Because not everything is an almost. When anything can happen, the worst often does.

It was May 2019 in Minneapolis, and spring was finally beginning to flirt with summer. Just a few weeks before, the sky had dumped two feet of snow across the Twin Cities, plunging us back into winter. But on this day, the weather army-crawled its way up to the temperate mid-seventies, and GrillFest was on. GrillFest is an annual event hosted by the state-centric glossy magazine, a gathering of people who want to try beers and grilled meats and fully celebrate the unofficial fifth season of the Midwest: patio season. A young father was scheduled to work and also had his four-year-old child, a slight inconvenience if you're financially stable and have a job with benefits, and potentially disastrous if you are an hourly employee hanging on to the edge of the poverty line. So this dad went to work and left his kid in the car with an iPad and the window cracked, and when his shift was over, so was his child's life. The newspapers reported on it, the story made it to my news feeds, and the commenters called for the father's head.

Terrible parenting

He should get the death penalty

No commenter seemed angry at God, or a country that had failed to prioritize the support of the family with childcare or a reasonable standard of living as a basic human right. Their ire was reserved only for the negligent parent whose poverty had made skipping work an impossibility, whose only means of supporting a child meant endangering that same child.

• • •

Anything Can Happen

Anything can happen. Depending on the day and our serotonin levels, this is either a promise or a threat. Around the corner there may be a new opportunity, new love, a great sale on the dress in our size and color. There may be a disaster, sickness, your sworn enemy right behind you in line on the day you decide "fuck it," and wear your crocs and sweats to the market. Anything can happen, and it does, but we cannot live every day with the awareness that we are small and fragile creatures, vulnerable spirits in inadequate vessels made of breakable bones and soft tissue. Parenthood in particular requires that we live in two realities; we must believe that the world will help us keep our children alive while also knowing that our environment is ambivalent at best, that something as small as a peanut or as large as an impassive body of water is all that stands between our child and death. There are things that no parenting book can prepare you for, things that don't come up in the Mommy and Me music classes or among your friends while you're all sharing tales of marathon bedtimes and skid-marked underpants shoved under beds for weeks at a time. Most of parenting is decidedly dull; a long slog of laundry and meals and wiping surfaces you just wiped, surfaces that seem destined to hold on to the grime and stickiness of life, surfaces that exist just to keep you busy, keep you wiping. Maybe it's this monotony that keeps us from crumbling under the weight of this uncertainty, that anything can happen and sometimes does.

The writer and rabbi Harold S. Kushner, author of the famed *When Bad Things Happen to Good People*, in writing about things just like this, said, "Why do we have to insist on everything being reasonable? Why must everything happen for a specific reason? Why can't we let the universe have a few rough edges?" The universe has plenty of rough edges, but we expect to be able to dodge them with the right accessories, the right education, the right situation. As parents, we're supposed to be the buffer between those rough edges and our children. And we are. We cut their food into tiny pieces, we fasten helmets beneath their heads and take them to their yearly doctor's visits. Sometimes we do what we're supposed to and it's still not enough. Sometimes, we *are* the rough edges.

Our friends from Minnesota came down to spend part of the winter in Arizona with their five beautiful children, who were in online school and craving sunshine and outdoor time that didn't mean putting on full snowsuits. Chelsey and her husband, Brandon, are the closest thing to perfect parents I've ever seen: creative and engaging and compassionate, and spending time with their family always makes me want to be a mom who does stuff instead of a mom who just watches stuff on Netflix. I hadn't seen Chelsey in ages, and while our husbands were firing up the grill and our children were playing quietly, she and I were having a tour of the various Arizona plants that are still alive in our backyard: a few mesquite trees, some agave, and a bougainvillea hedge that makes our part of the desert look lush and inviting. But I *had* to show her our neighbor's tree, a fully grown ficus that looks like a green hot-air balloon resting above their home. It's my favorite thing in the neighborhood, so perfectly shaped that a part of me understands those people you see on talk shows who insist they are married to inanimate objects. I don't know if this tree is single, but if it's reading this . . . I'm interested.

We stepped into the cul-de-sac, hands on our hips, and

that's when we heard it. A tapping. A slapping? A child's hand beating against the tinted windows of my car.

Babe.

I can't say I ran, because it was just a few steps. But I nearly tore that door right off its hinges, ready to admonish our four-year-old for playing in the car. He should know better! But he wasn't playing. His car seat harness was secured at his chest. His head was damp with sweat. He looked at me with love and gratitude, confusion and joy, his giant blue eyes wet with tears.

"Can I get out now?" he asked, and I felt the rough edge of the universe graze the back of my neck.

"I'm sorry I'm sorry I'm sorry I'm sorry," I whispered into his wet hair.

"I watched everyone go inside without me," he told me, clinging to my neck. "I called for you, and nobody comed back. Did you forget me?"

It had been an hour since we got back from our hike. We were four adults following nine children up and around winding pathways, urging the big kids to look out for the little ones, for everyone to keep an eye out for snakes, and to remember to drink their water and to stop when they got tired. At the end of the hike we were all dusty and the kids had formed alliances, and before we drove back to our house for dinner, we let them choose which car they drove back in. I turned off the car and took our stuff out of the trunk, and the rest of the kids in the car climbed over him and shut the door. It's true that *nobody* noticed he was gone, but it's also true that *I* didn't notice he was gone. That I left the car without him. That a part of my brain was so far away from where we were that I left our child in the car on a winter night in Arizona, where the temperature was only a few degrees cooler than it was for that little boy waiting for his father to finish his shift at GrillFest.

The grown-ups spent the rest of the night staring at all our children, sharing in the horror of what had happened, and the uneasy relief of what had not. Everyone but Matthew tried to assuage my guilt.

"I went out to our car twice and didn't hear him!" Brandon insisted.

"Anyone could have done this," Chelsey assured me.

But she was wrong, because Matthew would never make a mistake like this, just like all those internet commenters wouldn't have. Just like some of you reading this wouldn't have. Babe spent the night drinking electrolytes and clinging to me on the couch. That night, I insisted that he sleep with us. I kept him tucked into my armpit, my entire body tuned to the rise and fall of his chest and the ticking of his heart beneath my hand, imagining a tiny coffin and a funeral that marks the end of my marriage and the beginning of the hard drugs his siblings would start using immediately.

"I'm sorry," I whisper to Babe, but also to Matthew, who is lying with his back to me.

"I know," Matthew says coldly.

I googled "what to do when your kid goes through something really scary and it's your fault but really should your husband be *this* angry with you and could he maybe just try to have some compassion because you want to dissolve into a puff of smoke?" I texted my friends who work in psychology and mental health. And I spent the next few days telling Babe that I was sorry, asking him to tell me what happened and validating his story. He was four and very verbal, and hearing his tiny Muppet voice say, "Mom and all the kids got out of the car and I felt very sad and I called for you and nobody heard me and you forgetted me and I was scared and then you comed back and you showed me how to unbuckle my own car seat so I can never get stuck again!" Well, that didn't feel great, but it probably felt better than being stuck in a hot car alone while everyone else was inside playing *Mario Kart* and drinking pop! What struck me is that he had the story right, right away. He saw everything for what it was, without judgment. But he sensed my own judgment, maybe from how I winced at his telling of the story, or how I regularly capitulated before him, kissing the soles of his feet or his bare chest, telling him how much I love him. He told the story over and over again: to his day care teachers, to his grandmothers, to his siblings. And every time, we sucked in our breath, slapped on a smile, and said, "Yes, Babe. That's what happened."

Months passed like this.

"Mom! Remember me!" He'd call out from the back seat when we pulled into our driveway.

"Mom! Remember when you got out of the car and forgetted me?" he'd remind me in the aisles of Target, loud enough that any other mom could and probably did hear.

Months passed when he said nothing at all, and I was sure that the memory had been replaced entirely with *Roblox* or the plot of *How to Train Your Dragon*.

Matthew is no longer seething with anger at me, but this almost will never be fully forgiven. It is the rock in our shoe, the pea beneath a pile of mattresses, the *time I almost killed our child with my mindlessness.* He can say he forgives me, sure, but I know better. In therapy, I work on forgiving myself. I imagine my best friend telling me this story, and what I would say to her:

It happens. It's okay. You're not a bad mom.

That would help if I was my own best friend, but I'm a frenemy at best, and when Allen isn't around, I practice a different kind of self-talk:

You're a terrible mother. You don't deserve these children. You left him in the car like a bag of groceries.

I whisper about this to a few other mothers, testing what it feels like to expose this wound to the open air. All of them reassure me that I am not a monster, and some of them lean forward and offer up their own almosts: children who picked up bread knives or choked on gum they shouldn't have had, who rolled off the couch, who were left at day care, or who pulled a plastic bag over their face and breathed in. We know the weight of this guilt, and we will carry each other's.

Babe's preschool is just a half mile from our house, and on slow days I get to pick him up. I walk the few blocks up to his classroom, carrying his scooter and his helmet, and wait for him to round the corner with his tiny backpack, which he waits for me to remove like I'm a maitre d' taking his coat. He scoots happily beside me, babbling on about everything that happened during his day. He happily narcs on all his classmates, so I know who is a biter and who "makes bad choices." But one day, as we're scooting along, he changes topics as suddenly as he brakes.

"Mom!"

"Yeah?"

Anything Can Happen

"Remember when you lefted me in the car?"

"Yes, I do."

"You need to forget about that, okay? You need to forget it."

I tell him that's very good advice, and he scoots away, brilliantly unaware of what could have been. He turns to smile at me with his gap-tooth grin, like my friend's son smiles from the prayer card that was distributed at his funeral, where his school-age brothers served as pallbearers for his tiny casket and we all wept and clung to our living children, swearing perpetual vigilance to protect them from the forces of chaos swirling about us: the open water beckoning them to come closer, the bean that could stick in their airway, the rogue cells that could multiply into cancer. That this boy of mine is alive is a stroke of unearned luck, a shiny penny plucked from the dark blacktop of an unfeeling universe. Tonight, he will fall asleep in the crook of my arm, and his heart will hammer its beat against my open hand, a reminder that we made it through another day. But tomorrow? Well. Anything can happen.

17

Anyone Can Do It

Jane Goodall was one of the heroes of my childhood: refined and rugged, dressed in head-to-toe khaki and living in the jungle among the beasts she would study, her hair pulled into a perfectly messy bun, a few tousled pieces framing her elegant face. Where other people saw animals, Jane saw something more. She lived among the chimpanzees and reported back to all us snobby humans that they weren't all that different from us after all: they used tools, communicated, lived in communities, and provided care for one another. Characteristics and habits that we thought of as particularly human, things that set us apart from *them*, were actually things that connected us *to* them.

I had no aspirations of becoming Jane Goodall, I simply admired her. I didn't imagine being the kind of person who could dedicate her life to any one thing in particular, and certainly not a thing that required me to do anything related to camping. And yet, I've found myself channeling Jane throughout my adult life: living among strange creatures, noticing their patterns, realizing how similar they are to me. The internet has made this hobby easier, but even without the ability to zero in on different subcultures through the comfort and distance of a screen, I'm entranced by the identities we carry and how they build community. When Aaron was sick with cancer, he bought tickets to see one of his favorite bands live. Slayer is a metal band, a bunch of bearded guys in black scream-shouting lyrics like the following, from their hit song "Raining Blood":

Raining blood
From a lacerated sky
Bleeding its horror
Creating my structure
Now I shall reign in blood

As a middle schooler who used to change the channel as soon as Marilyn Manson came on MTV *just in case* God was watching and got the idea I was into Satan, it's hardly the kind of music I'd voluntarily listen to. But I loved Aaron, and I loved going places with him, and so we spent hundreds of dollars to go to a theater on the very outskirts of Minneapolis to see Slayer live and in person. From the moment we stepped inside, I was transfixed: all around me were people in trench coats and dyed black hair, facial piercings and concert tees from decades ago. These were people for whom Slayer was not just a band but a community, not just a show but a shared experience. I spent the entire show facing the crowd, watching how they mouthed or shouted the lyrics, the way the strobing lights illuminated their awed faces, the absolute humanity gathering together for this music, this moment.

"Aaron," I shouted in his ear, "I love this!"

For "Raining Blood," actual (fake) blood rained from above the band, and I joined the hordes of screaming fans. I also bought a T-shirt.

For months now I have been lurking in a Facebook group developed by an influencer and dedicated to people longing to *become* influencers. I received my "exclusive" invitation to this group the way all exclusive invitations ought to arrive: via an advertisement on Instagram telling me that this is the opportunity I've been waiting for, an "offering" from a pack of influencers so passionate about their lives that all they want is to help other people achieve the same passion about their own work. The advertisement includes the words *impact*, *growth*, *strategy*, and *income* and includes a link to the registration for an online "summit" where each of these influencers—identified by their Instagram handles and headshots that show each of them laughing into the camera lens—will share their tips and tricks for how to find your voice, pursue your passion, and help you grow into the person you're meant to be. All this, available for free. Or, at least free of charge. You provide your email address, and access to all this information is yours. I typed in the extra email address I created just for these purposes and saved the date.

My interest was not pure, nor was it purely snark. It's very trendy to hate influencers, the way it becomes trendy to hate anything associated with women's interests: novels by women are "women's lit" or "beach reads," the term "basic" applies to a woman who likes things that are too mainstream, and when women begin to infiltrate male-dominated career spaces, the salaries drop. A part of me *does* hate influencers: hates that by watching a tour of an impossibly beautiful Mormon woman's pantry—did you know that you could tour a pantry? You can when it's eight hundred square feet and includes a second kitchen to keep the main kitchen a spotless set for Instagram photos—makes me despise my own beautiful home. I hate the commodification of connection and authenticity, a word that, like "classy," tends to imply that the user does not have it. Influencing has turned every person into a brand, a channel, a twenty-four-hour television show where you are the central character, and the content is made possible by our generous sponsors.

But there's another category of influencers altogether, ones who run Facebook groups like this, ones who seemingly exist to influence other influencers. It seems like a niche audience, but tens of thousands of people have signed up for this Influencer Summit. The names on the Facebook page, where the event will be hosted, are influencers from a variety of areas: people who are considered gurus in the realm of . . . actually, I'm not sure. The whitened smiles of each of our coaches—another term that seems to have lost all meaning with its overuse—beam down on me from a header image, and I clear my calendar and settle into my home office (bed. I work from my bed) to observe, and maybe to learn.

The first speaker is a white woman I've followed for years, with skin tinted orange by filters (she sells a set of presets for thirty-four dollars, so your photos can look exactly like hers) and self-tanner (she has an affiliate link if you'd like it) and a squinty smile. She refers to herself as "your pal, {redacted}."

Anyone Can Do It

For a few years, I listened to her podcast and read her emails. She was a "Boss Babe" and a "Mompreneur"—phrases and concepts I personally found revolting—but she promised real, tangible advice, keys to a kingdom I couldn't quite figure out. Twenty episodes in, I still couldn't figure out how she made a million dollars in affiliate income alone, or how she bought four houses in cash, but I didn't care. I *liked her*. I liked her smile and her overly tanned skin, the way her photos all cycle through a familiar cadence:

1. Her in underwear or a bathing suit, softly caressing her stomach rolls or laughing into the sunshine. The caption assures you that she too has insecurities and that your body is also beautiful.
2. Her holding her baby, recalling her fertility journey, sometimes with a branded tag to try the bracelet she is paid to post about. The caption assures you that it was worth the wait and that you are not alone if your own baby has not yet arrived.
3. Her, staring at a phone, posing in one of her homes. The caption reminds you that she too is just a busy mom staring at a phone.

Each post also includes a question or a request for the audience: What are *you* insecure about? What are *you* struggling with? What are *you* looking forward to this weekend? I know from listening to her podcasts that these questions are strategic: they encourage followers to leave a comment, a form of engagement which increases her relevance to the almighty algorithm. But the *comments*. The women pouring their hearts out about lost babies, crushed dreams, their hopes for a Saturday afternoon. These are not her friends (though she calls them such), but her customers.

They are a fandom participating in the performance, a mass of faceless people consuming her siren song, a parasocial relationship where the connection they have with her is entirely in their heads and phones. Their engagement fuels her standing within the app, which she can use to set prices for brand deals and to market affiliate links. The engagement builds trust in her, so that she can send an email and sell you a course on how to use Pinterest and build your *own* empire. It might look like influencing, but it feels like something else entirely.

The multilevel-marketing industry (direct sales companies where the independent salespeople are also compensated through commissions of team "recruits" who join their sales teams) exists in a similar alternate reality. Salespeople for a "clean" skincare line insist that there is unlimited opportunity for selling eighteen-dollar lipsticks to your friends and family, and for those same friends and family to join your team. You're not competing, you're collaborating! Surely your friends will stop impulse-purchasing nine-dollar lipsticks from Target and pick you to be their sole provider of makeup and skincare! Influencers who claim that their success can be easily replicated appear to be creating their own pyramids: insisting that the people who admire them can be just like them, and teach other people to be just like *them*, and on and on and on. The promise is not in the reality but in the possibility.

At this morning's summit, this influencer is "teaching" from one of her beautiful homes, beaming down into her laptop camera and telling her origin story: how she too was once a corporate drone. How she learned everything she knows from Google and podcasts and books by experts, and then turned that knowledge into a whole other business, teaching what she learned for free in online courses that range from a few dollars to a few thousand dollars.

"If even one person follows you," she says with a smile, "*you* are an influencer."

She encourages people to think about what they can teach, what *they* are an expert in. I've heard this all day, and from other people like this: the limit does not exist, there is room for all, the market is endless, the only limit to your income is what you *want* to make.

I'm sure it feels like anyone can do it when you have a self-reported six-figure affiliate income from your nearly one million followers. But that math doesn't work for people with just a few hundred or even a few thousand followers. The idea that there is a market for *every person* on this livestream to be an online teacher of their own course material defies all economic and common sense.

Jane Goodall would not—I'm guessing—hate-watch an online conference, but that is exactly what I do with my entire day. I've spent treasured hours of my own life watching speaker after speaker smile into their professional video setups in their expensive homes, encouraging people who struggle to spell the word "entrepreneur" (myself included) to ditch their day job and work for themselves. In the days and months after the event, I watch these tens of thousands of people attempt to turn their passion into profit, the group filled with new posts every time I log in. *What business name sounds better:* Cure MS with Your Mind, or Your Mind: The Cure to MS? I think both are a great option if you'd like a lawsuit for practicing medicine without a license, but the group throws out other suggestions.

What stands between you and your dreams? Nobody replies to this one, or to most posts. I wonder if most of these people have given up and decided to keep their day jobs. I hope that they have. I want to warn these people against pursuing what they say is their dream because I transitioned from working in branding to being—and this term is repugnant to me—a *personal brand.* Everyone has a personal brand now, because it's not enough to simply have a job or a life. Your dentist sends an automated email reminding you to rate and review her on Google, Yelp, or wherever else you like to leave detailed recaps of the personal issues that require professional intervention. Your best friend has an Instagram account dedicated to her dog, and she only posts between seven to nine p.m. "when her audience is most engaged." The language of marketing and advertising—brand story, positioning, mission statement—have been co-opted and applied to people now. It was hard enough to sit around a conference room table earnestly trying to explain the "brand voice" of a discount haircut chain, but we personalized the kind of household goods you hardly ever think of, desperate to make our clients believe that yes, people are buying your glue because they are personally and emotionally attached to the brand promise of American Quality, not because they're hoping to bond together a broken object. We worked around the clock to make sure that you felt as though your favorite discount store had earned the kind of loyalty you'd previously reserve for a friend who held your hair back as you expelled coconut-flavored rum into your dorm room's toilet. We "leveraged" "user generated content" and helped to create influencer marketing that is now influencers marketing to their own market how to become a part of influencer marketing. The snake is eating its tail, and while I'm not sure what exactly late-stage capitalism is, I've read enough headlines to tell me that I think we're here. The irony is that for all the personality a brand is said to have, all the hundreds of millions of dollars that are poured into the theater of personification, a brand is nothing but a rigid set of standards: a logo paired with standard fonts and colors and tagline protected by armies of litigators, copyrights and trademarks. A brand is nothing but consistency designed to sell.

People are messy, unpredictable, and prone to taking things personally, on account of being persons. It would be *easier* to be a brand, to have a clear set of parameters on what we can or cannot do or say or think or wear. Certainly at least some of the appeal of the personal brand is the depersonalization of our actions and interactions, the way it makes it easier for people to dismiss or damage each other as though we're just avatars or ideas. On the other side of the laptop, that influencer is just a person. Her biggest insecurities and fears cannot be packaged into content or sold as life lessons. They are folded up somewhere inside her like the notes she probably passed around in middle school.

Jane's biggest discoveries about chimps proved how similar they were to people. My own discovery from these months of lurking is that I am the same as every person in this group and logged onto this summit; the same, probably, as many of these teachers. We are all desperate to know that our work and our lives mean something. We want to know, as we stand in a crowd crying out our favorite lyrics while fake blood pours from the ceiling, that we too are being heard.

18

Something Substantial

The writer Annie Dillard wrote "How we spend our days is, of course, how we spend our lives," a beautiful sentence that is freshly ruined for me every Sunday when I receive my weekly screen time report. I've kept a journal nearly my entire life, a documentation of my thoughts and feelings and comings and goings, but still the most accurate assessment of how I am spending my days and my life is this, the adult version of a report card: a notification on my phone telling me how much time I spent on this device, and when. Should I choose to click through—and I try not to—I can see what exactly I was doing while staring into the abyss of the screen. This report is somewhat new, and a reaction to all the bad press that technology has been getting lately. Not only is it responsible for eroding our democracy and sense of decency, for skewing election results and our perceptions of beauty, but it could, depending on what you read, be making you more anxious, dumber, and lonelier. We've been saying this about children for years: the American Academy of Pediatrics told us that children under two should not have any screen time, a report obviously written by somebody who has never tried sitting on a cross-country flight with an eighteen-month-old who wants to spend those hours in the sky running wind sprints down the aisle. But now, it turns out, even adults can be affected by these addictive devices that are attached to our person nearly twenty-four hours a day, one little rectangle that is an alarm clock, a television, a radio, a DJ, a camcorder, a camera, a Rolodex, a journal, the sum total of our personhood saved to the cloud.

The solution, of course, is *awareness*. And I am now *aware* that I am spending an average of five hours and twenty-four minutes on it every day, or approximately half of my waking hours. The good news is that that number is down 18 percent from the previous week. The bad news is this report does not include the time I spend on my computer, which I am seated in front of for what feels like at least seven hours a day. I tell myself that the number *is* slightly skewed, since it counts using the Maps app while driving, or the Podcast app while I'm taking a long walk through our neighborhood and only *sometimes* pause at the corners to check my Instagram. It counts things like phone calls, which are not the same thing as scrolling through your feeds, letting the warm waters of dopamine lap at the shores of your brain.

I opted into the screen time report to prove to Matthew how much time I wasn't spending on my phone, to illustrate to him just how balanced a relationship I have with technology. I imagined myself reviewing the numbers with him, oozing self-satisfaction. Perhaps he would even apologize to me, his virtuous and very present wife, for the times he's told me,

Something Substantial

"You're on your phone quite a lot." These numbers should terrify me, should shock me awake and inspire me to move to a rural community and live off the land, finding connection and meaning in growing carrots that become scraps for the chickens whose eggs become my breakfast and whose shells become fertilizer to grow more carrots. But instead, this number becomes the fertilizer that feeds my shame: when Mary Oliver asked rhetorically what we intend to do with "our one wild and precious life," she herself was rising early and listening to birds sing, immersing herself in the love of her partner, creating without checking the Amazon reviews. Good for her, I guess.

This is how you stay informed, I tell myself while I scroll through the news. I am *informed* that planes filled with desperate people are rolling down runways with more desperate people running alongside, hoping to hitch a ride away from something terrible. I am *informed* that there are vast and immeasurable pits of human suffering everywhere you turn; that while I am sitting on the toilet until my legs fall asleep, there is a mother on the other side of the world praying that her home isn't bombed. I have all the information available in human history sitting in my pocket, and I would fail any eighth grade quiz on World or American History.

This is your job, I tell myself while I tap in Instagram captions or reply to comments. It might not be my job, but it's surely adjacent to it. The hope—unproven as any other—is that this online attention will turn into real-life reward. That someone will remember my heartfelt caption about motherhood and make a beeline toward their local bookstore to buy a book by the woman who wrote that one caption. It sounds insane to say out loud, but sadder to say what I think is true: I'm addicted to my phone. But what's even sadder, objectively, is to not say it out loud at all but to have an ad on your own phone pose the question:

Are you addicted to your phone?

It's not a rhetorical question, there is a link to an online quiz that asks whether I *think* I spend too much time on my phone (yes), whether I lose track of time on it (yes), whether I use it while I should be focusing on something else (sorry, I was just on my phone while writing this sentence).

Physician Dr. Nzinga Harrison is an addiction expert and podcaster who told me that we get *something* out of our addictions: comfort, escape, a momentary burst of joy or dopamine. Our addictions do serve a purpose, even when they are simultaneously destroying us. We started drinking or taking pills or checking our phone obsessively for a reason, because we were looking for something.

I have always been looking for *something*. The internet arrived at Fifty-Third and Humboldt when I was in fifth grade. The ad agency where my father worked was upgrading their computer system, and our family got a screaming deal on the Apple computer where my father had spent the past two years writing ad copy for fishing lures or accounting firms. The computer was set up in our semi-finished basement, with linoleum floors likely adhered with some form of asbestos and water-stained walls. Our family desk was a heavy oak library table purchased from a yard sale at my mother's childhood library, with decades of chewed gum decorating the underside.

Something Substantial

The internet was delivered on CD-Roms from America On-line, who promised 200 FREE HOURS of internet access. We weren't sure exactly what the internet was, but my mother demonstrated this for us, dragging the mouse to the desktop and double-clicking on the triangle-shaped icon labeled AOL. As long as the phone line was clear, clicking on that triangle set off a Rube Goldberg-esque series of activities within that ancient computer, which hummed and clicked and finally announced your arrival on The Internet. Here, with every click, there was something new: a group of strangers to chat with about Laura Ingalls Wilder books or Nickelodeon shows, forums upon forums of people represented by screen names and avatars, a bazaar of entertainment and information that lasted until my brother picked up the telephone upstairs. I had my very own email address and could send messages to anyone on the internet. I sent my mother emails that said "I LOVE YOU" and eagerly checked my inbox later for her replies. The people I chatted with—mostly adults, which we now know is gross and weird and not okay—were interested in what I had to say, which only made me more eager to share.

My own screen time report, when compared with the general public's, is—allegedly—average. The statistic I find—that 46 percent of adults report using their phones for five to six hours a day—seems likely to be underreported, the same way so many of us tell our doctors that no, we've never smoked a cigarette, or that we drink maybe once a month, and never more than one drink a night. Still, five to six hours a day is more time than I've ever spent on any other unpaid endeavor, hobby, or pastime. I'm still—one year later—on page eleven of my *Learn to Play Piano* book. When I haltingly tap out "Ode to Joy," my face contorted in concentration as my brain tries to connect symbols to actions, Matthew asks me, "What song is that?" I'm still—several years in—stuck on level four of my daily Spanish program. Were I to spend nearly a full weekday in concentrated effort at either of these things, maybe I'd be able to play "Ode to Joy" *and* sing it in Spanish.

Periodically, I'll try to recapture a version of my life without the internet, to sober myself from the influence of constant external input. I'll hand over my passwords to my friends or my husband and beg them to keep me locked out no matter what I say. But even without the Instagram app, I find myself seeing my life through those squares. I finish a book and imagine taking a photo of it in my lap; I write captions in my mind for photos and videos that aren't being taken; I imagine how this idea would be received, the kinds of comments that I may receive, the way it feels to scroll through a page of notifications calling me "smart" or "funny" or "beautiful." It is not the experience, or even the documentation of the experience, but the experience of the reaction to the documentation of the experience that I am looking forward to. This is how the technology was designed: to keep us wanting, to keep us scrolling, to keep us searching.

A Pew Research article crosses my screen titled, "7% of Americans Don't Use the Internet. Who are they?" And I know the answer. My family is Irish Catholic and expansive: I have first cousins I couldn't pick out of a lineup and more than a few of them have the same name, but my father's brothers have always been special to me. Uncle Denny was in seminary by the time my dad was born, an adult sibling whom my father remembered as either coming or going from something, popping into their parents' house for a few weeks at a time between getting his master's or his PhD, or taking teaching jobs in Ireland, at Notre Dame, University of Kentucky, Bradley. He is an academic, though not a snob, and the only reason I know anything about his professional life is because I googled it. Should you attempt to steer the conversation toward him or any of his accomplishments, he will deftly steer the conversation back toward you. I, of course, loved this. I mostly saw Denny at weddings, funerals, and the occasional Easter, and he was a captive and engaged audience. He referred to me as "Nora, dear" in his velvet voice, and spoke to me about C. S. Lewis as though my thoughts on *The Lion, The Witch and the Wardrobe*—"pretty good book, lots of hard words"—were as interesting as any scholar's. As a child who thought herself a writer on par with the uncle whose dissertation on Thomas Merton was published as a textbook, I had no reservations about sending him my own manuscript: a novel about my grandmother's cats, Gertie and Alex. Denny sent back my pages with earnest notes like "What a character!" and copyedits to indicate that my sentences did not require eleven commas. I did not know that he was taking time away from writing scholarly articles about Thomas Merton, and he never mentioned it. Whether I was with Denny or corresponding with him, I was his intellectual equal, respected and admired.

If you asked me about my family, I would describe them as "beloved," so it shocked me to realize that I had not seen this beloved uncle in six years, on the unexpected occasion of my cousin Tommy's funeral, where we stood in a circle in absolute shock, trying desperately to find something to say about something so horrible. And while my childhood is filled with memories of these beloved figures admiring me and filling me with confidence, my adulthood lacks any serious connection with any of them. I know the daily routine of a twenty-four-year-old Mormon influencer and mother of four, but I don't know what my uncle does on a Saturday afternoon? I spend over six hours a day on this phone and I haven't used it to call people I will long for after they die? Denny answers the phone—a landline—on the third ring.

"Nora, dear!" he sighs, and I am once again a little girl, delighted to once again be the sun in his universe.

A few weeks later, my mother and I are sitting in the living room of my aunt Theresa's house, waiting for Denny to arrive for the first day of a three-day visit with no real agenda but for me to ask questions and listen.

"I'm sorry I'm late," Denny says, removing his hat at the front door. "I was distracted reading the most brilliant article." I wait, hoping the article will be something that I too have read, but the article that had him waylaid was a philosophy journal that I'm certainly not subscribed to, and whose premise I can only vaguely follow.

Because I'm a podcaster, I brought my recording equipment. It's a small recorder and a shotgun mic, but Denny sits down on the couch and after some pleasantries tells me kindly and sincerely that he is a private person. I am instantly embarrassed. He is a private person not in the way that a famous person might declare when in the midst of a PR crisis, but in the truest sense: his life is his. A microphone, a camera, a long-lost niece sitting on the floor with a pair of head-phones on—none of these are opportunities. I tell Denny that I understand, of course, and that this recording is just for me. I am here to ask him questions about my father—his baby brother—to mine for versions of him that live in the other people who knew him. And we do talk about my father. Denny recalls an image of his youngest brother as a toddler, his hair recently bleached by his older sisters and his skin tanned nut brown by the summer sun and offset by a pair of silver swimming briefs. The family was on vacation at Lake Delton, Wisconsin, laughing while their littlest sibling tried to run down the sun-beaten dock without burning the bottoms of his pale feet.

The microphone on the table is forgotten, and we talk the way people are meant to talk with those they treasure: in complete sentences and expansive thought, connecting anec-dotes and memories to larger meaning. How fascinating is it to know that fifteen years before his little brother arrived in Vietnam to fight a war, Denny would leave in peace after a tour training the Vietnamese navy on the operation of mine-sweepers, that their two different experiences in that one country were determined by power-hungry older men playing Monopoly with the world and the people in it? How comfort-ing is it to see my father's nose on his face, to see what might have been had my father not spent his years in Vietnam inhal-ing cancerous defoliants and smoking free Lucky Strike ciga-rettes. We talk through lunch—sandwiches wrapped in wax paper that my mother delivers to the living room from a local co-op—and we are not talking about my father anymore, we are talking about Catholicism and whether women could ever be priests, about the meaning of democracy and Plato's belief in the philosopher king; we are in agreement on almost nothing, but we pull out each other's thoughts and feelings, regard them with respect and move through our discomfort and onto other topics, other ideas. I have the distinct pleasure of explaining to him that one of the most popular fiction books of recent history was a love triangle between a virginal teenage girl, a 117-year-old vampire, and a teenage werewolf. He is incredulous and writes down the name of the author to look into later, not on the internet, but at the library. We roam through the house, settling in the sunny dining room and the wood-paneled den, and we cover the years between us effortlessly.

"I haven't had a conversation like this in a long time," I tell him. "It's really wonderful." He wonders whether this isn't the kind of conversation that could happen on the internet, and the only word for the sound that comes out of my mouth is a guffaw. Because no, this is not what happens on my version of the internet, where opinions are either inconsequential (what does your coffee mug really say about you?) or authoritative, loud and devoid of all nuance. Denny does not answer questions he doesn't know the answer to, he asks more questions. And when we finally notice that seven hours have passed since we first sat down, he suggests we meet up again for dinner in an hour and a half. It is on the five-minute drive back to my hotel that I realize I have not touched my phone all day. I wonder, nearly immediately, what I should post about this day. When I return home to Phoenix, I realize that the recordings are nearly unusable. A faulty microphone cord creates a tinny buzz around every spoken word, and a faulty operator recorded fourteen hours of conversation that registers as barely more than a whisper. It really is just for myself, and yet here I am writing about it, turning it not into a caption but into another kind of content entirely, synthesizing my experiences for the consumption of other people, for my own benefit.

Every week, the screen time report arrives bearing the same bad news about my days and my life. So too does a letter from Denny, the envelope bearing his beautiful cursive. I read them all in his voice, which I hear when I call him on the weekends. I send him my podcast, burned to CDs. He sends me a poem written just for me, which I tuck into a journal. We share an inside joke now, a phrase he repeated both nights he took me and my aunt and my mother to dinner, dressed in a suit and bow tie while our fellow patrons wore variations on cargo shorts and flip-flops. He was worried that the three of us might skimp on our orders, denying him the opportunity to really treat us.

"Now," he said that night, handing out the menus and inadvertently handing me a directive for a better life, "I want you to find . . . something substantial."

19

Good, Better, Best

Mrs. Ames told me I was special. Not in so many words, but I could tell by the way she beamed at me as I flew through *The Berenstain Bears and Too Much Junk Food* that I was a prodigy, a gem, the kind of kindergartner you only meet once in a lifetime. I'd had yet to read *Matilda*, but when I did, I would feel a sense of recognition in the title character whose teacher (major spoilers ahead) becomes her advocate and eventual adoptive parent. My other classmates were struggling with multisyllabic words, clapping their hands to help them understand the cadence of reading aloud, but I was flying through every book she put in front of me, shooting my hand up into the air before anyone else had a chance. I was specifically trying to beat out Troy, my only rival, who had a large skin tag growing like a mushroom on the side of his face and once told the class that I was poor because I was wearing a rug to school. *It was a kilt, Troy. A kilt.*

My teeny tiny small-town Catholic school didn't have a program for obnoxious children who got all their self-esteem from highly subjective measures of intelligence, but by second grade my family had moved to the big city of Minneapolis, Minnesota, and *that* Catholic school did. It was called SOAR, an acronym that stood for . . . *something* . . . and met in the windowless basement of our ancient building, above the staircase where the regular kids went sailing down to the sub-basement that doubled as a gym *and* a nuclear fallout shelter.

At first, I was one of the kids tumbling down that second staircase, gazing longingly into a room I most certainly belonged in, disappointed that Mrs. Ames had apparently not sent advance word about my superior intellect. Instead, I had to sit in the ordinary classroom and hope that when the teacher called on me, she would understand that I was special, that I had my own shelf of books at home, chapter books with no pictures that took place in olden times when children were dying of cholera and parents were simply Ma and Pa.

Weeks went by, maybe months, and twice a week I watched as a select group of my peers—including our school receptionist's son, I noticed, bristling at the obvious nepotism—went down to their secret lair while I had to play Bombardment and War and other more violent variations of dodgeball in a scratchy nylon uniform dress.

Each year, our parochial school participated in the same statewide testing as public schools, an entire three days spent sitting in silence, flipping through flimsy workbooks printed on gray recycled paper, and carefully filling out ovals with a freshly sharpened #2 pencil. I examined every pencil beforehand, certain my parents were going to ruin my future by slipping in a #3 pencil, or maybe a #4. I'd never seen any of these pencils, but one can never be too careful when one is about to be evaluated by a series of computers. Our parents were instructed to pack us special snacks to help power our brains, which was not a concern during any other part of the school year when we were allowed to eat only at lunchtime. Mrs. Boerner sat at her desk in the front of the classroom while we scratched out guesses to multiple-choice questions about short stories and math problems. To help our concentration, the bells in our school were turned off, and Mrs. Boerner's honeyed voice telling us "Pencils down" was the only indication that time had passed.

The results arrived in a larger-than-normal envelope, on tissue-thin paper that my mother opened unceremoniously, scanning over it briefly before dropping it onto the table with the catalogs and the various coupon flyers from local retailers that we never got around to redeeming. I grabbed it hungrily, my eyes racing to the right side of the page, which didn't just tell me how I did on the test but how well I did compared with my peers—if you could call them my peers, given that the numbers showed I was better than most of them. I was in the top percentiles, the upper echelons; I was about to SOAR. I imagined walking back into school, my bony shoulders pushed back, my head held high, intentionally hanging back when the rest of the kids lined up for gym class, knowing that I wouldn't need to worry about dodging any balls or touching any toes. I'd be in the SOAR room having intellectual discussions about the intricacies of Gertrude Warner's *The Boxcar Children* or maybe the brand-new Gulf War America had just gotten into. Perhaps we'd be creating historically accurate dioramas or learning the cello. I *was* special. I *was* chosen. I *was* . . . deeply disappointed once I made it into that room. My peers were just a bunch of second graders who happened to learn quickly but had the same intellectual depth as any other eight-year-old. They weren't in that basement room reaching for higher knowledge, just talking about Teenage Mutant Ninja Turtles between vocabulary games.

I did not admit that to anyone, instead perpetuating what I hoped was an air of mystique around the entire SOAR program, changing the subject when the regular kids asked what we did during SOAR time, acting like it was really as interesting as I'd always imagined it to be. I was not about to relinquish my specialness for anyone, not when I'd had to claw myself into the experience. I was the only person who seemed to notice just how not special we all were, how we were actually no smarter than anyone else in our grade. The SOAR label stuck with all of us through the rest of our time in grade school, marking us as smart and special. In a time before algorithmic marketing and data tracking, I don't know how the word got out about my specialness, but soon I was being invited to summer camps with kids from all over the city who bore variations on my same label. We wrote poetry and songs and created art, and at the end of our ten business days together, we wrote our parents' home phone numbers on scraps of paper we tucked into our pockets, promising to stay friends forever. Naturally, I never spoke to any of them again.

I know they're out there, though, those children from camp and SOAR, or whatever their school district's equivalent was. Like me, they've developed a dependence on the elixir of accomplishment and approval, and they're still hooked. Told that we could do *anything*, we heard "you must do everything, and do it perfectly." We quit sports when it was clear we weren't going pro, we dropped classes in college that threatened our GPA, and now we are the kinds of colleagues who buckle under the slightest amount of criticism and cannot help but poison the present moment with the arsenic of our own ambitions for the future. Without additional honors courses to take or secret camps to attend, we've had to find new ways to get high on the idea of being special: we've become Pinterest moms who produce professional-looking birthday parties for their barely coherent infants or small-business owners who write think pieces on entrepreneurship. We're authors who check their Goodreads reviews as though a detailed three-star review from a man who finds memoir "narcissistic" is a form of oxygen. My friend Hans once told me—straight-faced—that he is only as good as his last interaction, that his sense of self-worth rests precariously on the email response from a colleague or the driver who reaches the stop sign at the same time. A friend who has climbed to the literal top of one of the biggest corporations in the world calls to tell me that they feel empty and aimless, that every Sunday evening feels like walking the plank. I'm only as good as my next achievement; I allow myself anywhere between five to eight minutes of happiness about any accomplishment before shifting immediately into what's next, and how I can make it better. We are all exhausting, gaping holes of need trying to fill the void with perfection and progress and the pursuit of more and better, aching for a sheet of gold-star stickers and a grown-up to tell us that we belong here.

• • •

The walls of my youngest's preschool were lined with quilts. Some depicted Bible scenes like Noah's Ark filled with smiling pairs of animals apparently nonplussed by the aquatic destruction of their world, others featured Bible verses stitched into the patterns. But there was one I tried not to look at, and which I would have torn down from the wall and stuffed in the trash can had it not been in the view of a security camera. Next to the door for the Teddy Bear room, stitched in red across a plain linen panel in an otherwise loud patchwork quilt was a short rhyme:

> *Good, better, best.*
> *Never let it rest.*
> *'Til your good is better*
> *And your better is best.*

The quote was unattributed, but a cursory Google search pins this atrocity on Saint Jerome. While you cannot trust quote attribution on the internet (I'm so sorry to break it to you, but Audrey Hepburn was not the quote machine Pinterest would have you believe), I am about to renew my membership to the Catholic Church so I can petition to have Jerome un-sainted. *Never* let it rest, Jerome? *Never?* What if your best is just . . . bad? What if your good is good enough? What if you can't get into SOAR or Odyssey of the Mind or Model UN?

How do we keep all of the icky slime of our self-loathing from wiping off on our small, sweet children who do not care what anyone thinks of us, or what our GPA was, but who are already learning to value themselves according to the evaluations they've received? I do everything that Google and the parenting books I've skimmed suggested. I praise their efforts more than their achievements, I let them make mistakes, I whisper affirmations into their ears as they fall asleep and make them repeat them to me in the mirror: *I am good. I am smart. I am learning. I am doing my best.*

At eight years old, Ralph is skeptical of this practice.

"Mom," he says with an eye roll *in his voice*, "I know this already."

But if he knows it so well, then why is he crying about a worksheet? The worksheet in question is a math worksheet with fourteen problems involving the addition and subtraction of loose change. He got twelve of them correct.

"I got two wrong!" he wails with a sorrow so deep I wonder if maybe this *isn't just about the math worksheet.*

"What's going on, bud?" I ask, pulling him close to me like a dad in a '90s sitcom, gearing up for some background music and a heart-to-heart where maybe he asks me about his dead dad. He tenses and looks at me with incredulity, "I GOT TWO WRONG, MOM!"

So it *is* about the worksheet, I guess? But it's also a canary in my parenting coal mine, and I'm on high alert that he might already be poisoned by the gases of perfectionism and performance that have sickened me over the years. I don't get grades handed to me on a sheet of printer paper anymore, I'm graded daily and publicly, and I've cried plenty of tears over the adult version of 12/14 on a math worksheet. That constant feedback loop is a job hazard for me, but anyone who exists with even the vaguest online presence is vulnerable to this public review system, a constant assault on your perceived personal value based on likes or comments or friends or followers. What started as gold stars on our papers and being named Student of the Week in the weekly school newsletter is now LinkedIn connections and promotions and achievements we can wave publicly, proof of just how special we are. What can we do when a kid cries over missing two answers on a math worksheet other than try to shout down that persistent voice inside them chanting, *Good, Better, Best, Good, Better, Best*? But what child is dumb enough to believe you, knowing that their own school has special rooms for gifted kids, that they've already begun to be sorted by arbitrary measures of ability before they can even tie their shoes?

I get *the email* on a Thursday afternoon. I'm particularly open to suggestions during the afternoons: I'll click on any ad, read any email, take any digital rabbit hole away from my actual work, even when that email comes from my child's school. I'm not a parent who feels a particular urgency to click into the online portal and review my child's schoolwork; his best drawings make it home eventually and who am I to critique his handwriting? School feels like *his* domain, a place where he should feel freed from my gaze and my evaluations. This email's subject line was "Congratulations," so, anticipating an update on a silent auction item I didn't remember bidding on, I opened it. It was an invitation for Ralph to join the school district's gifted and talented program, based on the standardized tests he'd taken earlier in the year. I felt a small thrill, similar to the one I'd felt at his age when I saw my own standardized test scores. What I say about my child—that he's smart and capable and special—is now being validated through a sterile statistical model! The programming is described in this email as "rigorous" and "challenging" and designed for the district's brightest students. I delete it, and the reminder email that they send a few weeks later. If this is a huge parenting mistake, the only good news is that I won't know it for at least another twenty years, when it's too late to do anything about it and he's working on his first memoir. Maybe Ralph will be bored to tears in his regular classroom with all his friends. Maybe this choice will be all that stood between him and an exceptional life. I hope so.

I hope that all my children live free of any rhyming aphorism that encourages them to keep striving when it's clear that C's not only get degrees but produce C-suite executives. I hope that they are all dead average, that they go to whatever college they can afford without taking on massive student loan debt and pursue whatever job it is that helps them support a life that is unremarkable and unaccomplished, that they fall asleep believing that their efforts were enough and wake up feeling the peace of knowing that their worth is innate and endless. I hope that their happiness springs from within them naturally like well water, that they let it spill out of them and into the people around them, that they see themselves and others for who they are, not what they can do. I want this for my kids, and for all of us who are constantly seeking the next gold star, the next accolade, more proof that we are good and special and deserving of the space we take up on this planet.

I am not a quilter, but I am a writer, so I rewrote that rhyme with all due respect for Saint Jerome or Audrey Hepburn or whoever actually said it. May these words bring you comfort the next time you find yourself reaching for the next rung instead of thinking, *Huh, why exactly am I on this ladder anyway?*

> *Good, better, best.*
> *Give it a rest.*
> *Your good is probably fine.*
> *You don't need to be the best.*

ACKNOWLEDGMENTS

I t is inevitable that when you make a list of people to thank, you will forget one vital person, kind of like how I left my brother, Austin, off family emails for years . . . not because I didn't love him, but because I loved him so much I guess I assumed that he knew everything by osmosis or telepathy? To avoid this kind of mistake, I thank whoever is reading this. Without you, I would be nothing. I would have nothing. This book would not exist and I would be just energy floating through the ether.

I am able to write and create in part because I have the kind of partner that men have had for centuries: a husband who anticipates my needs and wants and arrives in my office in the morning with a breakfast burrito and a coffee, and a few hours later with whatever he knows I want for lunch. A man who books the kids' dentist appointments and finds me a power strip that is functional and beautiful and gives it to me for Valentine's Day. A man who folds my underwear and makes our house and our life and the world more beautiful. Matthew, I love you and I am grateful for the ways you have

Acknowledgments

made every one of my successes possible . . . and sweeter. Our beloved children give me endless inspiration and grace, and yes, I fear the day they become writers.

My family of origin—or what's left of it, ha!—has always given me great material and just the right amount of turbulence to keep life (and my work) interesting.

Jess Regel has been my agent since 2015, which means I've been with her longer than I've been with Matthew. Jess, thank you for seeing something in me when nobody else did, and for making sure my best ideas see the light of day and my worst ideas are immediately deleted from my computer.

Julia Cheiffetz edited this book and my very first, and always pushes me further than I thought I could go. Julia, I admire you as a person and as a professional, and I am so glad to be at the level where I can lie on the couch with your dog while you manually edit my manuscript with a marker. I am lucky to have you.

My best friend, Dave Gilmore, has been my first line editor for two decades, and he read many, many versions of every chapter in this book. Dave, I love you so much. Thank you for getting my jokes (and sometimes making them funnier).

Hannah Meacock Ross is a friend who has always brought out the best in me, particularly when I'm at my worst. Thank you for spending hours on the phone with me like it's 1997.

Marcel Malekebu, Jeyca Maldonado-Medina, Jordan Turgeon, and Megan Palmer are the team at Terrible, Thanks for Asking. I can step aside to write other things because they are creative partners who keep the train on the tracks. Working with all of you is an honor, and I treasure what we've made together.

Acknowledgments

I wrote parts of this book at the Buckhorn cabins outside Grand Rapids, Minnesota, at Changing Hands bookstore in Phoenix, and on many couches.

This book was copyedited by Stacey Sakal, who caught many grammatical mistakes and other embarrassing things. Thank you for making me look 10 percent less dumb!

ABOUT THE AUTHOR

Nora McInerny was voted Most Humorous by the Annunciation Catholic School Class of 1997. Since then, she's written the bestselling memoirs *It's Okay to Laugh (Crying Is Cool Too)* and *No Happy Endings: A Memoir*, as well as *The Hot Young Widows Club* and *Bad Moms: The Novel*. She hosts the award-winning podcast *Terrible, Thanks for Asking*, has spoken on TED's mainstage, and has contributed to publications like the *New York Times*, *Time*, *Slate*, and *Vox*. She is very tall.